Mr Collins Considered

By the same author

*Shakespeare's God: A Theological Criticism
of the Great Tragedies*

Mr Collins Considered

Approaches to Jane Austen

Ivor Morris

Routledge & Kegan Paul
London and New York

First published in 1987 by
Routledge & Kegan Paul Ltd.
11 New Fetter Lane, London EC4P 4EE

Published in the USA by
Routledge & Kegan Paul Inc.
in association with Methuen Inc.
29 West 35th Street, New York, NY 10001

Set in 10/12pt Sabon
by Inforum Limited, Portsmouth
and printed in Great Britain
by St Edmundsbury Press Ltd
Bury St Edmunds, Suffolk

Library of Congress Cataloging in Publication Data

Morris, Ivor.
Mr. Collins considered.
Includes index.
1. Austen, Jane, 1775–1817—Characters—Mr.
Collins.   2. Austen, Jane, 1775–1817—Criticism and
interpretation.   3. Collins, Mr. (Fictitious character)
4. Clergy in literature.   5. Social ethics in literature.
I. Title   II. Title: Mister Collins considered.
PR4038.C47M67   1987   823'.7   86–20266

British Library CIP Data also available
ISBN 0-7102-1005-1

To
A.J.N. and C.V.H.

Contents

There is in human nature generally
more of the fool than of the wise.

Francis Bacon (*Essays*, xii. 'Of Boldness')

Preface

The main purpose of criticism, and perhaps its only justification, is to send the reader back to the author's work with renewed interest. Next, but a long way behind, comes the offering of perceptions which the critic hopes will make possible a better understanding of the writer's intention and art. If this study of the inimitable Mr Collins achieves the former aim, it will show itself to have been worthwhile; and should it afford any enlightenment in the process, so much the better.

Jane Austen is the most impersonal of novelists. She does not write from the standpoint of her own feelings or reveal the climate of her thoughts: the autobiographical element on which so many rely is excluded. Her manner profoundly affects the novels. To turn their pages is not to discern the dawning of a light that never was, on sea or land. Her stories, and way of telling them, give little sense of imagination unbounded – of the plenipotent gaze which beckons into being a unique world with its peculiar atmosphere and its own laws, forbidding and baffling comparison. The bright, calm ordinariness of the scenes she presents to us is deceptive, though. A powerful imagination is in play; but it expresses itself, while concealing itself, in the objectivities of structure, plot and incident, as well as in masterly grasp of motive. Like all novelists, of course, she is the creator of individuality: it is the nature of her concern with situations in which individuals find themselves which distinguishes her from others.

The stories comprehend particular groupings of men and women, and the patterns of their interrelationships; each person, each family, each community has that integrity of existence which only great writing can bestow. Yet it would be true to say that Jane Austen is equally at pains to specify the exigencies of social living with which her people are at all times confronted, and which remain in essence unchanged – and in detail largely so – amidst the flux of events and the changefulness of life and personality. Their demands, be they of loyalty, of customary usage or of morality, constitute the warp to the weft of the characters' experience. For this reason it has seemed appropriate to treat the novels together in determining the groundwork of social convention and assumption, and in studying someone like Mr Collins, who is to be judged almost entirely on the basis of his public attitudes.

What is sauce for the goose, however, is sauce for the gander. The things by which the conduct of a Mr Collins is measured can be applied to that of others in *Pride and Prejudice* and the rest of the novels. This book does so apply them: it undertakes a close comparison of actions and sentiments of the main persons with his in similar situations. The result is that the clergyman of Hunsford (who, following in the style of his noble patroness Lady Catherine de Bourgh, very much likes to be useful) becomes a means of perspective through which the motivation of many characters may be reviewed, and fresh insights gained into the quality of Jane Austen's writing.

Particular acknowledgment is due to the observations of Margaret Kennedy and Lord David Cecil, which, apposite and challenging in their different ways, have proved invaluable in the framing of this work.

The text referred to throughout is that of R.W. Chapman's *The Novels of Jane Austen*, 3rd edition, Oxford University Press, 1932–4.

I should like to thank Mrs Vera Darvell, Mr and Mrs Charles Thomas and Mrs Shirley Young for assistance they have very kindly given.

Ivor Morris

1

Query

There is no one quite like Mr Collins. Not that he surpasses many other mild eccentrics of fiction in carrying the stamp of individuality. But his name has become a byword for a silliness all of his own – a felicitous blend of complacent self-approval and ceremonious servility. Like Mr Bennet, we listen to him with the keenest enjoyment; and while sparing sympathy for the presumable effect of being closeted in one's library with him until tea-time, we can never find the dose too much. If Mr Darcy and Elizabeth Bennet are a pair of literature's classic lovers, Mr Collins is surely one of its prize idiots.

He takes an honoured place in the comic tradition of healthy and robust ineptitude that produced a Costard and a Launcelot Gobbo; yet, though a retainer indeed by place and nature, he is not the cheerful nitwit blundering among his betters. Rather more elevated in ability and station, he makes his appearance as a lesser Malvolio, possessing much of the posturing steward's self-concern and sobriety, something of his hauteur, but little of his true stature.

Mr Collins is a cleric, but by no means an aspirant to sainthood, to judge by the habitual tenor of his ways. Neither is he devoted to idealistic causes in the manner of that more sterling source of merriment, Don Quixote – unless his 'kind intention of christening, marrying, and burying his parishioners whenever it were required' is to be seen in this light. Rather, Mr Collins is a mere attendant lordling, one who fills a place within the system. He steps assuredly into the novel as a civil servant of society, a sable-suited Dogberry with everything handsome about him – with more than two gowns, and gains rather than losses – uttering middle class maxims by great swarths, and displaying an adroitness in self-preservation worthy of the middle classes at their most unspeakable.

For there is nothing of Dogberry's fustian about him. He is a worthy son-in-law of that inoffensive mercantile knight Sir William Lucas, skilled in the lowly arts of advancement. Success, social and worldly, is within his reach, not solely through the odious entail which has made him heir of the Longbourn estate. Though born without the silver spoon he is on his way to achieving greatness, a measure of it having been thrust upon him by the chance recommendation to Lady Catherine de Bourgh. With a self-assurance born of vanity and insensitivity which renders him impervious to affront, Mr Collins directs his untroubled course past the disdain of the proud and the raised eyebrow of the perceptive, secure in the twin assumptions that are the bedrock of his being: the certainty of his excellence, and the necessity of his welfare. Among the less refined of society, both small and great, he makes a veritable Caesar's progress. To the Philipses and the Lucases, moved to awe at the excess of good breeding implied in his formality of speech and demeanour, he is 'a remarkably clever, good kind of young man'; by the de Bourghs he is deemed acceptable in the absence of proper company. Gauche, uncomprehending, even idiotic he may at times be – but his star is in the ascendant. Society repeatedly has taken his measure; but he has grown and prospered at society's expense. In the chronicle of literature's blockheads he must be set down as that comparative rarity, the Fortunate Fool. Our mirth, even at its height, is tempered by the disconcerting suspicion that he may yet have the last laugh.

When the matter of merriment is set to one side, though, the question does arise whether Mr Collins is a subject suitable for serious study. For as has often been remarked, he is a flat character. Margaret Kennedy, for example, would class him and his patroness Lady Catherine as 'two relics of the Little Character Monger period'. They are certainly entertaining, and models of their kind:

But they have strayed in from another book and are not quite worthy to be in a supporting cast with Elizabeth. This is particularly apparent in her scenes alone with them, when Mr Collins proposes, and in the final tussle with Lady Catherine. Elizabeth becomes a little less real when she is talking to them. She is three-dimensional and they are not. They put over character lines to which she must reply like a human being, and her own speeches become, in consequence, a little stilted.[1]

Elizabeth is however never more herself – indignantly and angrily so – than when she is responding to the verbal assaults of either party; and her taking on their accents in her answers might indicate a reciprocity rather than an artificiality in such passages.

But it has not always been customary to despise the flat character; nor, as a matter of fact, has Mr Collins always appeared as one. Anthony Trollope once denounced all the men in *Emma* as being weak: the Knightleys and Westons are 'simply sticks', he declares, in comparison with 'Mr Bennet and Mr Collins the immortal heroes of *Pride and Prejudice*'.[2] In more recent times Lionel Trilling, while aware of Sir Walter Scott's impatience with them as 'characters of folly or simplicity'[3], has defended Mr Woodhouse and Miss Bates as being remarkably interesting despite their having been created under a system of character portrayal no longer supposed to be valid: the displaying of a single trait in all their appearances.[4] A great writer, as is well known, can combine astonishing imaginative grasp with economy of treatment; could the commonsense observation of Elizabeth Bennet be as applicable in literature as in life, that 'It does not necessarily follow that a deep, intricate character is more or less estimable' than an uncomplex one?

What cannot be disputed is that Mr Collins is not the only male character in Jane Austen's novels existing by means of a simplicity of endowment or tendency and thus being short of a dimension. If we dismiss him on this score we shall find ourselves disposing of many. Take, for example, Edward Ferrars, the hero of *Sense and Sensibility*. Margaret Kennedy is not a whit less severe upon him than she has been upon Mr Collins:

he is a poor stick. He spends his time sitting about in low spirits, except on those occasions when he has not even the courage to sit. Other people determine his fate for him; his mother bullies him, Lucy traps him and then jilts him for his richer brother, Colonel Brandon supplies him with an income and Elinor marries him.

The character of Colonel Brandon, as alternate hero, is dominated by the 'exalted, hopeless love' for his brother's wife which both occasions the situations he meets and gives rise to his own disposition.[5] Most readers would concur in this judgment, and that of David Cecil that these two lack life and individuality, and have been invented all too obviously to serve the purposes of the plot.[6] But to what extent does Edmund Bertram, the lover of those very unlike heroines Mary Crawford and Fanny Price, come alive as a person? With all his kind-heartedness and uprightness, he remains a cipher – so much so, that Miss Kennedy deems it one of *Mansfield Park*'s subtleties that Henry Crawford, had he been a better man, would have been the right husband for a woman of such fine grain and undeveloped capacities as Fanny Price.[7]

And what is to be said of the hero of *Emma*, the novel of Jane Austen's maturity? He is splendidly realised; but does he display the breath and pulse and complexity of life? Where the achievement is so considerable, it would be petty to look for faults. Mr Knightley is the gentleman epitomised and brought into activity within a setting all the more revealing for its being domestic. His manners are superlatively good: so simple, so manly, so much part of the person that his possessing them scarcely occurs to us until we see how firmly yet urbanely he can deal with impertinence.[8] In this regard he is a model of rectitude; but in being prompted to use such an expression, we should be less than honest with ourselves not to admit that the metaphor is applicable in its more literal sense. For he is viewed from without, and is in consequence to some degree idealised, and so can never come alive in the way his darling Emma does. If this be to lack a dimension, he lacks it.

Even at their best, the men of the novels fall short of the sentient humanity of the heroines; and at their least inspired they are as flat as pancakes – though a pancake, especially at the right season, is an acceptable dish. If Mr Collins is less than three-dimensional, therefore, he is amidst good company; and he has the added virtue among his peers of being amusing. But if the principle laid down by Lionel Trilling holds good, he enjoys validity, and the right to literary appraisal. The reality of existence which fictional characters may claim, Trilling maintains, 'does not depend only upon what they do, but also upon what others do to or about them, upon the way they are regarded and responded to'.[9] There can be no doubt of Mr Collins's ability to meet these conditions: his place in the plot of the novel and in the minds of its persons is assured. He can be said to exist, as other characters of fiction exist. It is the quality of his existence that demands our attention. Unusual he certainly is; and the charge of eccentricity, that can be brought against her own father by no less a person than Elizabeth Bennet, may with at least as great justification be levelled at Mr Collins. If we are correctly to appraise him, we have to consider the question whether his thoughts and actions are more extreme, and in their context therefore more absurd and unlikely, than are those of the other persons of the novels.

'My dear Jane,' says Elizabeth Bennet to her sister, 'Mr Collins is a conceited, pompous, narrow-minded, silly man; you know he is, as well as I do; and you must feel, as well as I do, that the woman who marries him, cannot have a proper way of thinking.'

This statement is thoroughgoing and scathing; it is as much a denunciation as an estimate; we meet here a finality of utterance. Nevertheless, we tend to agree with Elizabeth's opinion of Mr Collins: harsh though it is, it appears nothing other than the truth about him. But it is by no means the only positive comment that Elizabeth makes about men who enter her social sphere. She has found George Wickham, shortly to be revealed as slanderer, gamester, seducer, to be by far the most agreeable man she has ever met; and, dressing with more than usual care, enters the drawing room at Netherfield Park with the one object of conquering all that remains unsubdued of his heart. By the end she is preserved from marrying, but condemned to have for brother-in-law, 'one of the most worthless young men in Great Britain'. The man who does eventually become her husband, she addresses upon his first application in the same style of frankness and finality:

> 'your manners impressing me with the fullest belief of your arrogance, your conceit, and your selfish disdain of the feelings of others, were such as to form that ground-work of dis-approbation, on which succeeding events have built so immove-able a dislike; and I had not known you a month before I felt that you were the last man in the world whom I could ever be prevailed on to marry.'

It is noteworthy that in all three instances the reader can do no other at the time than agree with what Elizabeth says, and approve her for saying it.

Can we depend for our estimate of Mr Collins upon a person whose judgments prove to be so wildly inaccurate? Yet, to be fair to her, the entire female population of Longbourn and Meryton had fallen for Wickham's charms; and, as for Mr Darcy, not only had his public manner quickly produced a disgust which turned the tide of his popularity, but his conduct at close quarters had come near to deserving Elizabeth's reproof. About the true character of both men, however, she has been woefully mistaken. The latter half of the novel shows her reaping the whirlwind of her own shame and humiliation: earnestly indeed does she wish, in face of her family's uninhi-bited dislike of the man she loves, that her former opinions 'had been more reasonable, and her expressions more moder-ate!'

But Elizabeth has no cause for contrition over her judgment of the Bingleys. From the start she is disinclined to think well of Caroline and Mrs Hurst, distrusts their high-flown sentiments and predicts their dropping her sister's acquaintance. Here it is Jane who is deceived, and self-deceived, asserting that Caro-line is unable to impose upon anyone, and naively arguing that if the two women desire their brother's happiness they cannot plan to detach her from him. Elizabeth, her judgment here 'too unassailed by any attention to herself', wonders how, with her good sense, Jane can be so blind. Could it not be that Elizabeth's perception is meant to appear as sound so long as the emotions do not intrude? She is stated at the beginning to be more observant and of less pliant disposition than her sister; and though Jane's remonstrance at the disgraceful light in which Wickham's charge would place Darcy passes unheeded at the time, it echoes Elizabeth's first thoughts. Had she not herself wondered, listening to Wickham's tale, how Darcy could have descended to such inhumanity, how he could be friend to such a man as Bingley, and why his very pride had not imposed just ways upon him?

But accurate judgment requires principle, as well as clear-sightedness. Jane is the only person to allow for some circumstance unknown as Wickham's slander spreads; and though confessing herself 'a little surprised' at Mr Collins's proposing to Charlotte and being accepted, she urges her sister, again unavailingly, to take into account the happy couple's unquestioned deservings. This kind of logic Elizabeth finds too prosaic to be relevant; she scorns it and will pay no heed to it. Her assessments are made at a far higher pitch, the product not of a fine frenzy, but of a true critical spirit. Elizabeth Bennet, we are all aware, shares her creator's delight in 'Follies and nonsense, whims and inconsistencies'; might it not be that while engaged in making festival of Mr Collins's pompous obtuseness she has overlooked the human being — that the very brilliance of the satirical illumination which she turns upon him blots from her view, and from our own, some unremarkable but positive qualities?

Brilliance, and even harshness. For there is evident in Elizabeth, as in Jane Austen herself, a vehemence of liking and dislike as to both persons and opinions. When she sees Bingley's sisters relapse into indifference towards Jane after their expressions of concern at her illness, Elizabeth is restored, we are told, to the enjoyment of her original dislike. Her response when Wickham first mentions Darcy is to attest his disagreeableness loudly and with warmth. And her friend Charlotte Lucas, in tactfully suggesting at the Netherfield ball that Darcy might prove a pleasant partner, undertakes a thankless task: 'Heaven forbid! – *That* would be the greatest misfortune of all! – To find a man agreeable whom one is determined to hate! – Do not wish me such an evil.' Ruefully later on, after the contents of Darcy's letter have been accepted, Elizabeth admits to Jane the unreasoning and vainglorious nature of her initial hostility. 'It is such a spur to one's genius,' she confesses in self-derision, 'such an opening for wit to have a dislike of that kind.' In the earlier part of the novel at least she has tended to arrogate to herself the satirist's freedom, as well as his vehemence. Just as she had denounced Darcy to an acquaintance of only a few minutes, she is ready blithely to assure the same Darcy that Charlotte is one of the few sensible women who would have married Mr Collins, holding up to question her hostess's integrity in the process.

It may be because she is confiding in gentlemen and presumed mental equals that Elizabeth feels safe in her detractions. But something of the same overstepping of bounds is surely present in her celebrated contradicting of Lady Catherine's views on 'coming out' in the drawing room at Rosings. She attacks this social convention as uncompromisingly as it has been upheld; whether, in doing so, she exhibits in herself the 'delicacy of mind' which she accuses the custom of injuring is open to doubt. The twentieth century finds her admirable in defence of her family and unabashed devotion to truth concerning an antiquated taboo, and applauds her resistance to Lady Catherine's impertinent inquiries and barely civil pronouncements. But in years and in rank Lady Catherine is greatly her senior; and equally as hostess she is deserving of respect. If a measure of rebuke is implicit in her, 'Upon my word, you give your opinion very decidedly for so young a person,' and intended in the peremptory sequel, 'Pray, what is your age?' much could be said in its justification. Good manners might be held to have required from Elizabeth that moderation of tone, if not of opinion, which was not in evidence.

Ought the same to be said regarding her view of Mr Collins? Could it be that her satirical propensity, or exuberance in her estimation of people, might cloud or mislead our better judgment here? True, Mr Collins's speeches and actions have an unmistakable eloquence of their own; yet our impressions of him cannot be divorced from those of the heroine: to some degree we see him through her eyes. Are we unguardedly giving his words and deeds the significance that Elizabeth Bennet does? And should we be mistaken in doing so?

To this surmise, an answer will be forthcoming from the reader's own reflections. A silk purse is not to be made out of Mr Collins's sow's ear. And for better authority, were it necessary, the author herself could be cited. Her manner of introducing him is ominous: 'He was a tall, heavy looking young man of five and twenty. His air was grave and stately, and his manners were very formal.' His initial sentiments, in their presence, on the marriageableness of the Bennet daughters, and his own readiness to admire them without injudicious haste, speak for themselves. But even if they did not, the decorous solemnity of his accents would have proclaimed the man: 'The garden in which stands my humble abode, is separated only by a lane from Rosings Park, her ladyship's residence.' Could anything sound sillier? The way is thus paved for Jane Austen's own estimate, which immediately follows. Mr Collins, she tells us, was not a sensible man; and neither education nor upbringing had made good the deficiency. The humility of manner acquired in youth had been countered by the effect of sudden prosperity upon 'the self-conceit of a weak head', the result being 'altogether a mixture of pride and obsequiousness, self-importance and humility'.

Amidst the social routine it is soon evident that, despite his formality of utterance, Mr Collins has little to say. His talk with his young cousins is full of pompous nothings, and he is carried away from the Philipses at Meryton unceasingly affirming indifference to his losses at whist, enumerating all the dishes at supper, and apologising for the room he is taking up in the coach. Thanks and apologies make up the greater part of Mr Collins's conversation; but they are pursued with a punctiliousness which defeats the object of civility – as when he apologises to Mrs Philips for intruding upon her without previous acquaintance despite his cousins' presence with him, or regales Mr Bennet with promises of letters of thanks, or detains his visitor in the cold at the gate of Hunsford Parsonage with minute inquiries after her family. Out of his own mouth he is accused of the pompousness, narrow-mindedness and silliness that Elizabeth credits him with.

In setting out to visit Charlotte at Hunsford, Elizabeth is confident that she will meet at the Parsonage 'a man who has not one agreeable quality, who has neither manner nor sense to recommend him'. She finds there also a woman who appears to share her opinion. Charlotte had willingly agreed to an early marriage date, knowing that 'The stupidity with which he was favoured by nature' would render Mr Collins's courtship onerous. Her single purpose had been to secure an establishment; now, secure within it, she greets her friend with so cheerful an air that Elizabeth begins to wonder. Involuntarily she glances at Charlotte on those not infrequent occasions when she might reasonably be ashamed of what her husband is saying – and learns the extent of wifely wisdom in such a marriage. 'Once or twice she could discern a faint blush; but in general Charlotte wisely did not hear.' If for a moment we hesitate to accept from the woman who has turned him down that Mr Collins is a fool, we must surely trust the judgment of the woman who marries him – not to mention the writer who created him.

2

Compliment

If there is one episode, apart from that of his proposing to
Elizabeth, which may be thought to provide the best example
of Mr Collins's quality, it is the after-dinner discussion during
his first evening with the Bennets on the subject of his association with the family of de Bourgh. Having been raised to a
pitch above his usual solemnity of manner by the tribute to
Lady Catherine's affability and condescension, he makes as
near an approach to the lyrical as his pedestrian nature permits
when Mr Bennet asks if Miss de Bourgh has been presented at
court. The exchange merits being given in full.

'Her indifferent state of health unhappily prevents her from
being in town; and by that means, as I told Lady Catherine
myself one day, has deprived the British court of its brightest
ornament. Her ladyship seemed pleased with the idea, and you
may imagine that I am happy on every occasion to offer those
little delicate compliments which are always acceptable to
ladies. I have more than once observed to Lady Catherine, that
her charming daughter seemed born to be a duchess, and that
the most elevated rank, instead of giving her consequence,
would be adorned by her. – These are the kind of little things
that please her ladyship, and it is a sort of attention which I
conceive myself peculiarly bound to pay.'

'You judge very properly,' said Mr Bennet, 'and it is happy for
you that you possess the talent of flattering with delicacy. May I
ask whether these pleasing attentions proceed from the impulse
of the moment, or are the result of previous study?'

'They arise chiefly from what is passing at the time, and
though I sometimes amuse myself with suggesting and arrang-
ing such little elegant compliments as may be adapted to

ordinary occasions, I always wish to give them as unstudied an air as possible.'

Mr Bennet's expectations were fully answered. His cousin was as absurd as he had hoped.

If compliment be the food of absurdity in a literary character, however, what is to be thought of the real-life James Digweed, friend of the Austen family, and cleric to boot, who one day left Hampshire uttering native woodnotes which Jane felt obliged to communicate to Cassandra?

> I think he must be in love with you, from his anxiety to have you go to the Faversham Balls, & likewise from his supposing, that the two Elms fell from their greif at your absence. Was it not a galant idea? – It never occurred to me before, but I dare say it was so.[1]

Mr Collins himself could never have been guilty of such excess: while his tributes to ladies can scarcely struggle to metaphor, the flesh and blood Digweed joins animism to hyperbole. Anything that smacked of affectation was fair game to Jane Austen, we know. But do we heed sufficiently the fact that the artificiality of compliment was part of the convention through which men addressed women in her day? That James Digweed was not another Mr Collins – or, rather, that Collins is nothing but an aspiring Digweed?

It is hard for us to allow for the dictates of the manners of those times; and even harder to appreciate the restraints which governed relationship between man and woman. The paying of compliments was a way through barriers which have long ceased to exist. As well as being part of the ceremonial of courtesy proper to a gentleman, it was the counterweight to that restricted if not inferior position society gave a gentle-woman – an apparently enhanced respect masking what might today be seen as contempt.

A man's not having wit enough to offer compliments requisite to the occasion was a phenomenon as amusing to the author as the custom itself appears to have been. John Thorpe and Mr Rushworth come in for a kind of derision from which Mr Collins is immune. The former, having heard General Tilney call Catherine Morland the finest girl in Bath, accords her the 'delicate flattery' of passing on the compliment at second hand, confiding in a lowered voice, and as the height of endeavour in this mode, 'And what do you think I said? Well done, General, said I, I am quite of your mind.' Rushworth, the other resident beyond the Austen pale, wishing to acknowledge Lady Bertram's good taste in advising 'a very pretty shrubbery' at Sotherton, but also to insinuate that in his concern for ladies' comfort there is one in particular he wants to please, becomes lost in mid-sentence, and has to be rescued by Edmund proposing wine. What invention, however, is to be expected of someone who cannot learn his lines in *Lovers' Vows*?

Should we ask ourselves who, by contrast, is the most impressive complimenter in the novels, a surprise awaits us. We should never have assumed this type of accomplishment in the forbidding senior Tilney – but assuredly he is the man. If the General's deportment on the battlefield matches his prowess in the drawing room, he is fit to be ranked with none but Achilles. Few young women can have received tribute on the scale granted Catherine. The admiration of the elasticity of her walk, which so surprises her, is but a beginning. By way of being invited to leave Bath and stay at Northanger Abbey she is prevailed on to 'quit this scene of public triumph'. The Allens give permission for her visit; and, 'Since they can consent to part with you,' the General declares, 'we may expect philosophy from all the world.' The sentiment is Marlovian; and that which sends Catherine to her slumbers after her first day at the Abbey is in the spirit, and almost the phrase, of Alexander Pope. 'Can either of us,' he asks her, indicating his evening's reading, 'be more meetly employed? *My* eyes will be blinding for the good of others; and *yours* preparing by rest for future mischief.' But while malfeasance on the heroine's part is to confine itself to (not altogether unjustified) speculation upon the destiny of Mrs Tilney, the General will soon be drumming his visitor out of the house with martial fury: the master of compliment is to reveal himself as master also of insult.

Yet perhaps he has a rival in the gentler of these two social preoccupations. Magnificence can be oppressive; and though General Tilney can achieve what Sir Walter Scott might have called 'the big Bow-Wow strain' in this sort of thing, it is surely Frank Churchill whose compliments come closest to the ideal Mr Collins has enunciated: that they should arise chiefly from what is passing at the time, and have as unstudied an air as possible. Having made his appearance in Highbury as if in a state of rare enjoyment, Churchill speaks enthusiastically to Emma in approval of his father's marriage and praise of the former Miss Taylor, concluding that the family from whom he has received such a blessing 'must ever be considered as having conferred the highest obligation on him'. Jane Austen comments drily that he gets as near as he can to thanking her for Miss Taylor's merits. But almost immediately he is off again towards the periphery of praise: he expresses surprise at finding so pretty a young woman in his father's bride. Warned by Emma respecting the proprieties in the use of such a phrase, he assures her, with a bow, that in addressing Mrs Weston, he is aware whom he may praise 'without any danger of being thought extravagant in my terms'. The periphery is attained, by dint of a consummate change of direction. Emma, conscious of expectations that have been aroused in others and in themselves by their meeting, wonders whether these compliments mark Churchill's acquiescence or his defiance. She does not yet understand his ways, she tells herself – but the one thing she is sure of is that they are agreeable.

Compliment need not be an unnatural form of expression. It can suggest itself and be bestowed, in any age, upon the pure and simple promptings of the heart. We find it so in the world of the novels. Edmund Bertram, for example, touched by Fanny Price's rising to his defence in arguing the sermon's efficacy, and amused by the picture Mary Crawford then presents of a minister quarrelling with his wife all week but preaching himself into a good humour on Sundays by way of interlude, is moved to say, affectionately, 'I think the man who could often quarrel with Fanny must be beyond the reach of any sermons'. We warm to him at that moment – as we do to Marianne Dashwood when, understanding Lucy Steele's slight upon herself only as a possible reflection on the constancy of the mutely embarrassed Edward Ferrars, she urges with calm seriousness his modesty, generosity and trustworthiness, then rounds on him with, 'Edward, it is so and I will say it. What! are you never to hear yourself praised!'

Spontaneity is rare, though. Almost invariably we find the compliment being used with studied purpose, as a means to an end. Mrs Norris has perfected the technique of disarming with unexpected praise the intentions of those opposed to her wishes. Perhaps she has been forced to acquire it in sheer self-defence against the deliberation of Sir Thomas Bertram. However this may be, she is interrupting to applaud the generosity and delicacy of his notions as soon as he begins his objections to the idea of bringing one of the Price children to Mansfield Park. Lavishing commendation upon him as he gravely points out the responsibilities for the girl's later years that are implied, she promises upon breaking his train of thought that, under the impulsion of her own warm-heartedness, she will contribute all she can. Thus, with a liberality in praise which shakes the superflux to herself – the only charitableness she proves herself to be capable of – she attains her object. But good nature itself can resort to complimentary language for the ease and benefit of another. Edmund seeks to do away Fanny's fears that she is foolish and awkward by praising her good sense, sweet temper and grateful heart. Mr Bingley, aware of Elizabeth's pained reaction to Caroline's charge that she has pleasure in nothing but books, hastily intervenes with the more than kind, 'In nursing your sister I am sure you have pleasure', adding the hope of its increase through Jane's swift recovery. And Henry Tilney, in gently reproving Catherine for overlooking her jilted brother's hurt in her loyalty to Isabella, utters a compliment replete with humour. 'Your mind,' he tells her, 'is warped by an innate principle of general integrity, and therefore not accessible to the cool reasonings of family partiality, or a desire of revenge.' Catherine is charmed out of her bitterness. Captain Tilney cannot be so unpardonably guilty, she feels, while Henry makes himself so agreeable.

It is not often that compliments like these are of platonic inspiration. They are chiefly a means of recommending oneself to the opposite sex; and Henry Tilney is not at all averse so to using them. It is part of his purpose in the last example; but more memorable is the outcome of his thoughts when, during the interval of their two dances, Catherine innocently supposes it to be from kindness alone that Captain Tilney so urgently wishes to have the betrothed and seated Isabella Thorpe as his partner. She does not understand the comments Henry smilingly makes on her attitude; and having warned her that comprehension will involve her in 'a very cruel embarrassment', he explains when she insists that what she has assumed about his brother's motive proves her to be superior in good nature to all the rest of the world. These words show Henry to be his father's son; and their effect upon Catherine is to be noted. She of course blushes and disclaims; but there was a something in them 'which repaid her for the pain of confusion; and that something occupied her mind so much, that she drew back for some time, forgetting to speak or listen, and almost forgetting where she was'. Much the same occurs later when, having been teased into the recognition of being not much afflicted by the loss of Isabella's friendship, she is told, 'You feel, as you always do, what is most to the credit of human nature.' Jane Austen impishly remarks that 'by some chance or other' Catherine finds her spirits so greatly relieved by this conversation that she cannot regret having made the disclosure which led to it.

Yet these sentiments of Henry's still come from the heart: they are spoken with the directness of a fine nature and under the influence of a dawning love. In the more usual course of events, however, no real mutual sympathy need exist. The compliment is the disclosure – resolute or tentative, social or intimate – of a preference.

With calculated indirectness Willoughby addresses meaningful praise to the Dashwoods' cottage. It is, he declares, for him the only form of building in which happiness is attainable. The idea of structural alteration fills him with alarm. 'Tell me,' he cries, 'that not only your house will remain the same, but that I shall ever find you and yours as unchanged as your dwelling.' By this means he is enabled to declare his affection for Marianne without committing himself. In similar fashion, Henry Crawford first acquaints Sir Thomas with his purpose regarding Fanny Price by overtures for the renting of Thornton Lacey, his object, as he puts it, being to improve and perfect 'that friendship and intimacy with the Mansfield Park family which was increasing in value to him every day'. Sir Thomas thereupon carefully observes the behaviour of Crawford and Fanny, and finds the demands of decorum to be satisfied in the respectfulness of the one and the modest calmness of the other. None could doubt the meaning of Crawford's inquiry.

Livelier times are heralded when tributes become more directly personal, for then the compliment comes into its own as the prelude to romance. That such a day does not dawn for John Thorpe is something for which he cannot really be blamed: the desire to declare himself is present, but wit is wanting for the performance. Like Henry Tilney, he is attracted by Catherine's kindliness of disposition – but words and mind alike fail him in the very act of rendering praise:

> 'You have more good-nature and all that, than anybody living I believe. A monstrous deal of good-nature, and it is not only good-nature, but you have so much, so much of every thing; and then you have such – upon my soul I do not know any body like you.'

No such incapacity affects Mr Elton. He has the right word at the right time; and though Emma finds a sort of parade in his speeches which is very apt to incline her to laugh, there can be no doubting that proficiency, at least, in complimenting has been acquired. We remember him, perhaps unfairly, for rapturous exclamations like 'Exactly so!' or the 'What a precious deposit!' as he sighingly accepts Harriet's portrait parcelled for framing. But Mr Elton's commendations are otherwise intelligent and graceful. His congratulating Emma for Harriet's improvement is faultless in its nice balance of moderation and excess. Emma has given her all that she required in making her refined and assured: 'She was a beautiful creature when she came to you, but, in my opinion, the attractions you have added are infinitely superior to what she received from nature.' And his reference to Emma's visiting Harriet during her illness – he had flattered himself that she must be better after such a cordial as he knew had been given in the morning – has so much of aptness and humour that Emma would be boorish in shooting it down as she does, were she not incited by her protégée's supposed interests.

Whether more or less graceful, or more or less sincere, this kind of compliment is almost invariably recognised as an avowal. Even Mr Elton's mild charade has for Emma an emphasis that leaves her in no doubt as to his intentions. Elton is doubtless hindered by not being in love; for when a compliment proceeds from real feeling in a man of education and taste, its import is unequivocal: it has almost the status of a proposal. Such is the communication which Mr Elliot addresses to Anne in the concert room in Bath. He tells her that he regards her as one 'too modest, for the world in general to be aware of half her accomplishments, and too highly accomplished for modesty to be natural in any other woman'. Her response, not surprisingly, is confusion; and within moments she is being informed of the charm her name has long had for him, and of his wish that the name might never change. This is no trifling. Mr Elliot has declared his love in the complimentary style in which avouchment could properly be made. It is thus not at all surprising if Anne has earlier been roused to alertness, if not to alarm, by her father's urging Mrs Clay to remain with them and meet the beautiful Mrs Wallis, with the words, 'To your fine mind, I well know the sight of beauty is a real gratification.'

In *Pride and Prejudice*, Darcy makes his proposal in form – but it is at the second attempt. The first has taken place some days previously when, calling upon Elizabeth at the Parsonage in the absence of Mrs Collins and Maria, he finds himself in desultory dispute as to what constitutes an easy distance to be settled away from one's family. Suddenly he draws his chair nearer to her and says, '*You* cannot have a right to such very strong local attachment. *You* cannot have been always at Longbourn.' There is no fine language here. The compliment to Elizabeth's sophistication has the simplicity and vigour which comes from strength of feeling; Darcy has seized the moment that offered itself – or half offered itself. But the lady's response is not what he had hoped. Elizabeth shows neither gratification nor consciousness, but surprise: the gentleman reacts sensitively, with a change of tone and subject: the compliment has not led to a situation in which he can declare himself. To the same unaffected utterance is Henry Crawford reduced by Fanny Price's rejection of his love. There is no hint of the pretentiousness, the verbal ingenuity of former praise in his last words as they leave the ramparts at Portsmouth. He asks her to put the statement 'I am well' in her letters to his sister; he knows she 'cannot write or speak a falsehood'. When he begs her in saying goodbye to advise whether he should go to Everingham and ensure that injustice is not being done to his tenants, she declines, saying he knows very well what is right. 'Yes,' he replies impressively. 'When you give me your opinion, I always know what is right. Your judgement is my rule of right.' His words will not avail, and he knows it. There is both manliness and despondency in their tone.

That Jane Austen's women are capable of compliment is apparent from Caroline Bingley's fond attentions to Mr Darcy. She distinguishes herself far less in the art even than Mr Collins. There is neither style nor subtlety in her flatteries; their purpose is all too crudely manifest, not least to Darcy himself. They amount to no more than indiscriminate praise – from the delightfulness of his library at Pemberley to the speed and evenness of his handwriting. Not content with championing any view he puts forward, Caroline makes assertions which transport compliment to the realm of adulation – and arouse the militancy of Elizabeth Bennet: 'Teaze calmness of temper and presence of mind! No, no – I feel he may defy us there. And as to laughter, we will not expose ourselves, if you please, by attempting to laugh without a subject. Mr. Darcy may hug himself.'

Just as undistinguished, but far more socially effective, is the manner in which Maria Bertram makes her feelings plain to Henry Crawford. There is a terseness almost wifely in the exhortation by which she sees to it that they will meet at Sotherton when he is there contributing ideas for its improvement. 'Those who see quickly, will resolve quickly and act quickly,' she tells him, in accents oddly reminiscent of Lady Macbeth. '*You* can never want employment. Instead of envying Mr Rushworth, you should assist him with your opinion.'

The higher flights of compliment are not to be sought in women when convention scarcely allows that an affectionate thought might enter their heads before the man has proposed. But neither is accomplishment to be found in men Jane Austen respects. If they speak in the mode at all, they do so plainly; but they usually dispense with it altogether. Should we suspect the absence of compliment in Edward Ferrars and Colonel Brandon to be due to their lifelessness, or that any initiative from Mr Darcy must be subdued by the sportive disposition of his beloved, we must be aware, with Mary Crawford, that Edmund Bertram, the most idealistic of the heroes, is not pleasant by any common rule, talks no nonsense, and offers a lady the compliment of nothing but tranquil and simple attention. While his brother Tom is busy felicitating Mary on showing the world what female manners should be, he settles the matter under discussion by observing in plain terms that girls whose behaviour changes abruptly on their coming out are simply 'ill brought up'.

Though Captain Wentworth might appear to verge upon compliment in his earnestly advising Louisa Musgrove to cherish the qualities of mind she has displayed, he never actually does compliment a woman – except, perhaps, in the fervency of composing the letter to Anne that will decide his fate. Almost the same is to be said of Mr Knightley. He gives compliments to none – certainly not to Emma, who receives from him criticism, and even reproaches. Yet perhaps it is in keeping with the ways of the society Jane Austen knew that in proposing to Emma – an unpremeditated action to which he is driven by his feelings – he makes use of the complimentary form to express an admiration we must allow to be deserved: 'You hear nothing but truth from me. – I have blamed you, and lectured you, and you have borne it as no other woman in England would have borne it.'

Sentiments of like moment, Mrs Collins is destined never to hear from her spouse; but his compliments, it is to be hoped, will not be entirely reserved for the inhabitants of Rosings Park, but will find a domestic application. It is doubtful if Charlotte will be told that she is born to be a duchess, or that she has it within her to become the brightest ornament of the British court. But any offering she may receive within this kind will be a similarly commonplace affair. Mr Collins's compliments are not imaginative enough to be striking; indeed, they can seem merely part of a deferential manner. That such conduct is demanded by Lady Catherine, however, and that Mr Collins's apparently unstudied tributes bring gracious smiles from her, is a fact perfectly unremarkable in the novels' world. For what is absurd in Mr Collins is not that he spends time and thought in fashioning compliments, or even that he is bad at it – but that he admits to doing it.

3

Mediocrity

The epitaph composed in jest for Charles II applies almost in reverse to Mr Collins. On a number of occasions he does wise, or worldly-wise things, but he is persistently guilty of saying foolish ones. If his pronouncements are not inept in manifest want of wisdom, they will be judged so in their dullness. For he is, undeniably, a bore; and he lacks the minimal merit, possessed by a Robert Ferrars or a John Thorpe in their obtuseness, of being able to startle or to affront: his attitude, always ingratiating and apologetic, robs him of any such saving vice. Nor does he enjoy anything like Harriet Smith's advantage of being a pretty and underprivileged young woman with a flair for romantic attachment – for Harriet, too, is by no means a giant of intellect.

Dullness in Mr Collins is unrelieved. What more do we ever learn from him than that Lady Catherine is condescending, that young ladies should not scorn useful instruction, that resignation to misfortune is assisted if the object which was sought loses its appeal – and that the duties of clergymen are such as he will itemise with zeal upon any opportunity? But dullness, though a social disadvantage, is not altogether contemptible; how can it be, when it is strongly evident in so many worthy persons in all walks of life? We surely owe it to Mr Collins to investigate whether his evident absurdity arises less from within than from contrast with the environment in which he finds himself; whether, in fact, he is silly by comparison rather than through innate genius.

That the comparison is stark – that Mr Collins is time and again put into the shade by the sheer winsomeness of the life the novels display – cannot be denied. What could a Collins ever have to do with the affectionate and lively intelligence of the elder Bennet sisters? He is permanently exiled, we must think, from such reaches of the human spirit. Even at the somewhat lower level of relationships at Netherfield, marred as they sometimes are by touches of ill-nature, Mr Collins would still be an outsider: in no way could he contribute to the mature assessments of people, opinions and affairs that form part of the discussions amongst Bingley and his sisters. In the brilliance of the Crawfords he would be able to do nothing but blink, never comprehending the 'right of a lively mind' to seize whatever contributes to its own amusement, or that of others. The wit that can daringly compare Maria's situation upon the reappearance of Sir Thomas Bertram to the Greek heroes offering sacrifices to the gods on their safe return, or picture itself as offending 'all the farmers, all the labourers, all the hay in the parish' in requesting the use of a cart at harvest-time, would hold no sense for him. Mary Crawford, indeed, would have enjoyed Mr Collins more than Elizabeth did: her humour, being tolerant and thus more pure, would not have admitted the elements of irritation and annoyance that are present in Elizabeth's reaction.

Examples abound of a range of experience for which the mind of Mr Collins is simply unfitted. We might recall Henry Tilney's cultured charm and sense of fun as he assures the two girls, while they stroll round Beechen Cliff, that no one can think more highly than he of women's understanding: 'In my opinion, nature has given them so much, that they never find it necessary to use more than half.' Or it may be Captain Harville speaking 'in a tone of strong feeling' of the sailor's thoughts as he watches the boat containing his wife and children as long as it is in sight, then turns away wondering if they will ever meet again – states of mind outside Mr Collins's cognizance, if not his capacity. What, we might wonder, would he make of the Navy's conviviality – of Captain Wentworth's bantering seriousness upon the Admiralty's vagaries, or of his professed gallantry towards women which makes their presence on his ship 'an evil in itself', and their finding comfort on board an anathema? Or would he in any degree appreciate the bond of tenderness and sympathy at Barton Cottage which unites the Dashwoods? Certainly, that extreme of delicacy in Mrs

Dashwood which will refrain from asking a daughter if she is engaged for fear of provoking conflict between filial duty and womanly discretion, and the quizzical humour which causes her with grave kindness to inquire of a young man whether he is still to be a great orator in spite of himself, would alike hold no value for someone of Mr Collins's coarser clay.

Yet instances like these, agreeable though they be, do not typify the novels' world. Far from it: they are exceptions which prove the rule. The Bennets and the Dashwoods, it must be remembered, are on the fringes of society, as are Captain Wentworth and his Navy associates; the Crawfords, though personable, are parvenus – a fact which might explain Henry's custom of never putting himself in a position of inferiority by asking questions, or his respect for the appearance of gentlemen's residences; and the Bingleys and their friend Darcy represent the younger generation of great houses or affluent families. The scenes in which they are involved – the brightness and appeal of the relationships there depicted – are not characteristic of the society Jane Austen presents to us. As Anne Elliot appears to have been only too aware, such moments are more in the nature of oases in a desert of mental aridity.

If one tried to recollect what General Tilney actually has to say in *Northanger Abbey*, compliments and remarks relating to his domicile apart, one would be in difficulty because it does not amount to much. His personality is chiefly distinguished by its inhibiting speech and sociability in others. Catherine, visiting in Milsom-street, finds Miss Tilney more reserved than hitherto, while Henry has 'never said so little, nor been so little agreeable'. She cannot at this stage ascribe his children's want of spirits to the father's presence, though unaccountably, because of his unfailing courtesies, she feels it a release to get away from him. Only at the Abbey does she become conscious of the restraint he imposes, despite his charming ways; his departure for London confirms the impression, and gives her 'the first experimental conviction that a loss may be sometimes a gain'. The reader arrives at this point before Catherine, having been perhaps forewarned by the General's angry impatience with the waiters and discontent at whatever the inn at Petty-France afforded. The spectacle of his pacing the drawing room at the Abbey, watch in hand, and pulling the bell with violence at the instant of her entering to command 'Dinner to be on table *directly!*' cannot however fail to make his guest acquainted with the domestic tone.

The other substantial household in the book is that of the Allens, who own the chief of the property about Fullerton. Mr Allen, its head, is by contrast a retiring sort of man, mainly, one must suspect, because of Mrs Allen, who has refrained from dying in the manner of the jointress of Northanger. She might just as well have followed suit, if the worthwhileness of her remarks be the criterion. From her one may learn that the streets will be very wet if it keeps raining; that open carriages are nasty things, inimical to clean gowns; that Fullerton is eight miles, not nine, from Salisbury. Umbrellas, she informs us, 'are disagreeable things to carry. I would much rather take a chair at any time.' Her husband is a constant source of puzzlement to her. He had rather any thing in the world than walk out in a great coat; she wonders that he should dislike it when it must be so comfortable. Equally strange is his talk of being sick of Bath, for it is so very agreeable a place, and he is quite in luck to be sent there for his health. Self-centred though she is, Mrs Allen is redeemed from self-sufficiency by the fortunate repetition of, 'How glad I am we have met with Mrs Thorpe!' Evidently even she is in danger of being overcome by the tedium of her own society. When Catherine confides to Henry Tilney that, at home in the country, she 'can only go and call on Mrs Allen', his reaction is amusement. ' "Only go and call on Mrs Allen!" he repeated. "What a picture of intellectual poverty!" ' His words are proved only too just. For what is this lady's response at the theatre when her young charge, assuring Henry in her sorrow at the broken appointment that she would ten thousand times rather have been with him, turns an ardent face to her in appealing for her confirmation? It is the bewildering, 'My dear, you tumble my gown.'

Mr Allen is not completely negligible. He shows decision in

making for the card room as soon as they arrive in the assembly hall, and diplomacy in diverting any blame that may attach to his wife for seeming to have sanctioned Catherine's being driven about in the carriage of a young man unrelated to her. It is only on the latter practice, however, that he is heard to commit himself to an opinion. It is curiously negative – as dull in connotation as anything his wife has ever spoken: 'These schemes are not at all the thing. Young men and women driving about the country in open carriages! Now and then it is very well; but going to inns and public places together! It is not right; and I wonder Mrs Thorpe should allow it.' The speech dashes any residual hope there may have been for the intellectual climate of the Allens' menage.

And what of Mansfield Park? It can be the abode of no light-heartedness, social or intellectual. The stateliness and severity of its proprietor casts a constraint on all dwelling within its walls. Sir Thomas Bertram shares with General Tilney the distinction of being better appreciated in absence than proximity. On the occasion of his departure for Antigua, Jane Austen tells us, his daughters were to be pitied, not for their sorrow, but for their want of it. 'Their father was no object of love to them, he had never seemed the friend of their pleasures, and his absence was unhappily most welcome. They were relieved by it from all restraint'; and the relief experienced by Fanny Price, what is more, is 'quite equal to her cousins' '. That the moment of his unexpected return is one of consternation, and even 'absolute horror', must be in large measure attributed to the iniquity, if not sacrilege, of the theatricals embarked upon in that mansion. But that there are other and deeper causes is clear from the alteration his government immediately imposes. Mansfield Park is soon 'all sameness and gloom, compared with the past'. Edmund's comment on the lack of animation moves Fanny to say that, as well as she can recollect, it has always been so, and their evenings were never merry 'except when my uncle was in town'.

Sir Thomas is a man of no mean intellectual ability. If its operation can, as it does, reduce relationship to formality and repress the feelings of those round him, one might be tempted to wonder if it can have like effect upon their minds. Can this be the cause of Lady Bertram's spending her days in quiescence, sitting nicely dressed on the sofa engaged in needlework? But perhaps it is her own weakness of intellect which makes her decide to ask Sir Thomas whether she can do without Fanny for the evening of the dinner party, or causes her, after a quarter of an hour's silent consideration, to respond to his gentle insistence on the necessity of children's leaving home upon their marriage with, 'I am very glad we took Fanny as we did, for now the others are away, we feel the good of it.' Her saying to the girl grieving under the threat of removal to her Aunt Norris's that it can make very little difference to her whether she is in one house or the other, seems to denote nothing less than a state of torpor; and the surmise is reinforced when Tom, arguing that the family's putting on a play would help to keep his mother's spirits up during the anxious weeks of Sir Thomas's voyage home, looks to her for support, and finds her just falling into a doze, 'sunk back in one corner of the sofa, the picture of health, wealth, ease and tranquillity'. The revelation of her niece's beauty can but summon up in her self-congratulation at having sent Chapman to help her dress before the ball – while joyous approval upon Fanny's receiving Crawford's proposal takes the form of the offer of a puppy 'the next time pug has a litter'.

Whether Lady Bertram is to be seen as the victim of Mansfield Park, or as resting on her laurels having won a stupefying victory over it, can never be determined. But it is certain that though Mansfield might subdue, it need not deaden: with a single exception, the life of the thoughts and emotions continues to pulsate beneath its ordered calm. Fanny's delicacy of perception and Edmund's moral idealism develop unhindered there. So do tendencies less edifying: the abrasive neuroticism of Mrs Norris, and the mordant passionateness of Maria. But there is small indication on the surface of what may be going on in the depths; incommunicativeness seems to be the rule for successful living at Mansfield Park, and its inhabitants are as a result largely strangers to one another. Visitors may bring bursts of animation, particular incidents may give rise to serious discussion; but the norm is the exclusion from conversation of everything save the commonplace. Mansfield,

Jane Austen tells us, is at most times 'a sombre family-party rarely enlivened'.

We must assume, from what the owner of the part-mortgaged Kellynch Hall has to say about the curate of Monkford, that he would never have admitted Mr Collins to the rank of gentleman. It is less certain that Mr Collins's pronouncements would be outshone by his own. Sir Walter Elliot has never been guilty of picking up a volume of sermons, either for his own benefit or to impress others. His reading is limited to a single book, the Baronetage; and his everyday reflections centre with 'warmest respect and devotion' upon the person in whom the blessings of baronetcy and beauty are united, namely himself. Thus, though he displays less reserve than Sir Thomas Bertram and greater readiness to talk at length, his utterances tend to be restricted to matters of rank and personal appearance, topics which are for him of all-consuming interest. Despite admitting the naval profession to be of some utility to the nation, he personally finds it offensive on the twin grounds of its bringing persons of obscure birth into undue distinction, while at the same time subjecting their appearance to processes of premature ageing which make them unfit to be seen and deserving of being 'knocked on the head at once'. The sentiment is somewhat redeemed by jocularity of manner; and Sir Walter is not above asking his agent whether the renting of Kellynch Hall will not be, for some wealthy naval officer, 'rather the greatest prize of all, let him have taken ever so many before – hey, Shepherd?' The jest's weakness need not be in his disfavour: a modicum of humour in dealing with one's inferiors is admissible, provided it is not overdone; but it is soon clear that the baronet has displayed the extent of his powers, both of wit and wisdom. His only other accomplishment, in which his daughter Elizabeth shares, is the ability to freeze a roomful of people into embarrassed silence by a parading demeanour of 'heartless elegance'.

From the Great House at Uppercross we expect something different, and are not disappointed. The Musgroves, we are informed, are 'a very good sort of people' (Jane Austen's phrase for the moderate): friendly, hospitable, not much educated and not at all elegant. So far, so good; but their normal pursuits, when we get to know them, are a degree less than auspicious. The men are busy guarding and destroying their own game, and otherwise engaged with their horses, dogs and newspapers; the women are fully occupied with house-keeping, neighbours, dress, dancing and music. The effect upon the cultured Lady Russell of what Mrs Musgrove terms 'a little quiet cheerfulness at home' amidst the family is to make her resolve not to call at Uppercross in the Christmas holidays.

The first we hear about Charles Musgrove is that he is out shooting. Sport is the only thing he does with any zeal, and his time is otherwise trifled away. His wife, like him no reader, makes it a point of indignation against Captain Benwick that when sitting over a book he will not take part in conversation or know 'when one drops one's scissors, or any thing that happens'. Stirrings of intellect, it is clear, are no more to be expected at Uppercross than at Kellynch; and any hopes there may be of Laura-place are quickly dashed. According to Anne Elliot, there is to be found in the noble residents no superiority of demeanour, accomplishment or understanding: they are 'nothing'. Lady Dalrymple by virtue of a ready smile and civil answer for everybody is accounted charming, and Miss Car-teret, 'with still less to say', is so plain and awkward that her birth alone makes her tolerated in Camden-place. In terms of mind and eloquence, therefore, Mr Collins would have been at no great disadvantage in any of the residences where the action of *Persuasion* unfolds.

The same of course applies at Rosings, where title does not foster the laconic. The custom there is for Lady Catherine de Bourgh to talk among her guests 'without intermission' on every subject in manner pontifical; and it is topic, no less than bearing, that gives rise to Elizabeth's distaste. Lady Cather-ine's inquiries, advice and instructions extend from her guests' employments, their servants, the disposition of their furniture and care of their cows and poultry to the size of their joints of meat and the packing of their trunks; so limitless and oppres-sively trivial are their aunt's concerns that Darcy and Colonel Fitzwilliam are driven beyond the range of her hearing, until they are called on to tell her what they are talking of. Colonel

Fitzwilliam shows a quite touching gladness upon Mr and Mrs Collins and Elizabeth's joining them for the evening at Lady Catherine's invitation. 'Any thing,' Jane Austen comments, with reason, 'was a welcome relief to him at Rosings.' Mr Collins alone is at his ease – in his glory, rather – finding solace, edification and pleasure unalloyed in the trite outpourings of his aristocratic patroness.

He would have fared no worse at Barton Park: what recommended him to Lady Catherine could not fail of its effect in the household where Lucy and Anne Steele so quickly become indispensable. Neither is the home of discernment; and at Barton, capacity itself seems to be lacking. In outward conduct Sir John Middleton and his wife are quite unlike, his vein of clamorous mirth being the antithesis of her cold insipidity; but that they strongly resemble each other in 'total want of talent and taste' is quickly established – during the Dashwoods' first visit, when Marianne is at the pianoforte. Sir John is loud in acclaiming every song, and as loud in his conversation while each is being sung. Lady Middleton, frequently calling him to order and expressing wonder that anyone's attention should be diverted from music for a moment, requests Marianne to sing a particular song which she has just finished. Husband and wife later entirely concur in condemnation of the fickle-hearted Willoughby. Exclaiming that he is such a good-natured fellow and as bold a rider as is to be found anywhere, he wishes him at the devil with all his heart. Lady Middleton, saying once or twice every day as the subject is raised, 'It is very shocking indeed!', is able to look upon the Miss Dashwoods with placid indifference, and in a short time with forgetfulness of the entire matter.

The Middletons find fitting companionship in the wealthy families they become acquainted with. The owner of Norland Park can discern in Mrs Jennings a woman of admirable comportment; and the meeting of his wife and Lady Middleton takes place, to the immense gratification of each, in 'an insipid propriety of demeanour and a general want of understanding'. The charmed circle – with the Miss Steeles, of course, in attendance – is completed by the head of the house of Ferrars, who in character is distinguished by 'pride and ill nature', in conduct by the 'mean-spirited folly' of her attitude to Marianne and her own sons, and in conversation by a judicious taciturnity. 'She was not a woman of many words: for, unlike people in general, she proportioned them to the number of her ideas.'

When all gather in the impressive milieu of John Dashwood's dinner party in Harley-street, the only instance of poverty that is noticed relates to conversation. All present labour under one or other of the disqualifications for agreeableness which Jane Austen specifies as 'Want of sense, either natural or improved – want of elegance – want of spirits – or want of temper'. While the gentlemen can fall back upon politics, enclosing land and breaking horses, the ladies are reduced to determining the comparative heights of Harry Dashwood and William Middleton – a subject affording them matter for energising speculation, especially since one opinion rates each to be taller than the other. But, in content and spirit, this party is not markedly different from others which the novels record. Apart from converse more or less agreeable with certain friends and acquaintances, what does Emma Woodhouse find at the Coles' party? 'Nothing worse', we are told, 'than every day remarks, dull repetitions, old news, and heavy jokes.' The society of Highbury is not as elegant as that of Kellynch Hall; but the latter's 'usual style of give-and-take invitations, and dinners of formality and display' stands no comparison, in the discriminating and sorrowing mind of Anne Elliot, with the natural hospitality among brother-officers of the Navy. And the private parties in which she is perforce included while staying at Camden-place she dismisses as 'elegant stupidity'. The phrase well describes the 'handsome' dinner, resplendent with plate and servants, to which Elizabeth Bennet is invited at Rosings. The party 'did not supply much conversation'. Miss de Bourgh says not a word, Maria Lucas thinks speech out of the question, Charlotte and Sir William are employed in listening to Lady Catherine. Mr Collins, taking his seat at the bottom of the table by his hostess's desire, and carving, eating and praising with 'delighted alacrity', is the only other contributor of talk at the meal; and his promptitude in agreeing, thanking and apologising provides the descant upon Lady Catherine's subsequent performance at the card table. He is in his element on that occasion, as the other guests are not.

Mr Woodhouse would not in the normal way be found at a party; and if he attends one, is too preoccupied with the subjects of draught, digestion and departure to heed what is going on or make any contribution to it. He is head of the younger branch of an ancient though untitled family; but, if it rested with him alone, sense would be entirely absent from his household. Of this fact Emma, though dearly loving her father, is well aware. She knows he cannot meet her in conversation rational or playful, or recommend himself to others by any talents whatsoever. The nearest he can get to conviction is a hatred of change of any kind, matrimony included; so obsessive is his anxiety over health that he can find fault with his darling Emma's portrait of Harriet sitting with only a little shawl over her shoulders under a tree, on what is supposed to be a warm summer's day – on the grounds of the subject's likelihood to catch cold. When he composes himself to sleep after dinner, as usual, Emma can only sit and think of the friend she has lost in Miss Taylor, now Mrs Weston, and of the 'intellectual solitude' by which she is threatened. Sleeping or awake, Mr Woodhouse can never admit rationality. His state of mind at the zenith of its powers reveals itself in his words to Emma after meeting Mrs Elton: 'Well, my dear, considering we never saw her before, she seems a very pretty sort of young lady.' What would have been his response to meeting Mr Collins? Emma would have feasted upon him; but is it to be doubted that her father, like Mrs Philips, would have been impressed and somewhat awed?

Silly as he may be, dull as he most certainly is, Mr Collins will always appear strongly contrasted to Jane Austen's lively and personable heroines and those attracted to them in affection and friendship. But with the society the novels present to us he is not unduly at variance; nor can he be said to be altogether disqualified, by personal gifts and, moreover, the lack of them, from advancement within it. For that society, with all its prepossessingness and glitter, can be seen to tolerate, even to encourage, the mediocre. Whether through the self-congratulatory arrogance of its leaders, the zeal for ostentation and general striving for elegance; whether through the rigours of decorum, and the demands of its formal manners, with their accompanying constraints and embarrassments; or whether through the intellectual shortcomings, native obtuseness or sheer ineptitude of those it favours with wealth and station, the society we are made acquainted with is rarely vivacious, usually downright dull, and occasionally vacuous to the point of stupidity. With his ceremoniousness of manner, and brain which can achieve little better than platitude, Mr Collins is not badly equipped to meet its everyday demands. In a number of respects he is better adapted to it than are some of Jane Austen's heroines.

4

Wealth

It is not only mirth that Mr Collins provokes, however, but disapproval. Whatever his personal attributes may be, his inclinations are to be regarded as more sinister. For Mr Collins is mercenary. In the very act of professing adoration to the woman of his choice, he makes a precise statement of his financial claim: 'one thousand pounds in the 4 per cents.' upon her mother's decease. Is not this despicable? Nor is it all: for he sees fit to add the astounding assurance to his beloved that no word of reproach for her financial deficiency will ever pass his lips after they are married. The fact that his love for Elizabeth is quite imaginary does not excuse him, any more than does his dressing it up in a desire – which he affirms to be most meritorious – to improve the lot of the Bennet daughters upon his inheriting the estate. The sentiment cannot hide his real concern with possession and his own advantage. So inebriated is he apparently with the thought of what he has to offer that he dismisses Elizabeth's refusal in sheer disbelief – and, when she persists, presumes to lecture her on the unlikelihood of her receiving another proposal of marriage because of the small-ness of her dowry. And this affront he commits in the evident belief that he is thereby recommending his suit. Only words like materialistic and venal, surely, can describe a mentality of this kind.

In all fairness to Mr Collins, though, the question should be asked whether there exists in Jane Austen's novels any think-ing on the subject of marriage which is unassociated with the mercenary. And the truth is that virtually none is to be found. Money – the need for it and the satisfactions of possessing it – forms part of the prettiest 'musings of high-wrought love and eternal constancy' entertained by any of the heroines. The phrase is used to betoken the gentle and principled mind of Anne Elliot – who eight and a half years previously has rejected, or been prevailed on to reject, the man she loved, upon considerations purely and solely financial. Her father had found the projected alliance degrading; Lady Russell had seen it as unfortunate that a young woman with her claims of birth, beauty and mind should be 'snatched off by a stranger without alliance or fortune', and determined to use 'any fair interference of friendship' to prevent it. Though strongly influenced by them, Anne nevertheless made her own decision, contriving to believe that she was 'being prudent, and self-denying' principally for Wentworth's advantage. She is somewhat of a conformist, admittedly; but Marianne Dashwood, the most romantically disposed of them all, and by conviction scornful of society's prescripts, views an income of two thousand a-year as being the smallest upon which an establishment proper to the married state can be supported.

That acquaintance with a gentleman should presuppose familiarity with his financial affairs, one might readily dismiss as a quirk of the imagination of someone like Mrs Bennet, stirred by happenings at Netherfield Park. Yet it is as true of Mr Bingley, Mr Darcy and Colonel Brandon as it is of Mr Rushworth, Mr Crawford and Captain Wentworth that the report of their income accompanies their personal introduction, and arouses just as much interest. More than this: it does seem a universal assumption from the way people behave that knowing a man implies knowledge of his bank balance. One is not surprised that a John Dashwood, suspecting a liking on Colonel Brandon's part for Elinor, should immediately inquire of her as to 'the amount of his fortune'; or, when Mrs Norris puts the idea of a match between Mr Crawford and Julia into her mind, that Mrs Rushworth should as instantly ask, 'What is his property?' and remark on his being a very genteel, steady young man only after this question has been favourably answered. But the same pattern of behaviour is to be observed in Eleanor Tilney. No sooner had she read James Morland's letter telling of Isabella's jilting him in favour of Captain Tilney than, expressing concern and surprise, she 'began to inquire into Miss Thorpe's connexions and fortune'. Significantly, wealth is the first consideration in Charles Musgrove's defence of Charles Hayter's character as a future brother-in-law, and the only one which will allow Edmund Bertram to tolerate that of James Rushworth. The former points out to his wife that Charles, apart from the something he might get from the Bishop in a year or two, will step into 'very pretty property' upon his uncle's decease; the thought that he is 'a very good-natured, good sort of a fellow' takes second place. Edmund is himself little impressed by wealth as such; it is perhaps the more revealing, therefore, that he cannot refrain from saying to himself in Rushworth's company, 'If this man had not twelve thousand a year, he would be a very stupid fellow.'

One is reminded of Lady Bracknell, who, having come upon the scene to find Jack Worthing unexpectedly proposing to her daughter, orders the languishing Gwendolen out of the room, impassively produces a notebook, and proceeds to question the young man on the state, not of his affections, but of his possessions. This scale of priorities, absurd in itself, represents the common attitude of Lady Bracknell's class – and, quite unmistakably, of the society which Jane Austen delineates.

Catherine Morland, in her innocence, is surprised to find Henry and Eleanor agreeing that Isabella's want of consequence and wealth must be an impediment to her marrying Captain Tilney; but she has learned something of the way of the world by the time she hears her mother declare that, apart from hurt feelings, her brother's loss of Isabella has done no harm: his marrying a girl 'so entirely without fortune' would not have been a desirable thing. Isabella herself, with greater realism than her friend, had been pessimistic as to the Morlands' consent: 'I dare not expect it; my fortune will be so small; they can never consent to it.' Isabella's perception is not denied Elizabeth Bennet, but her resignation is. Angrily Elizabeth tells her sister that they are not rich or grand enough for the Bingleys; and Colonel Fitzwilliam's disclosing Darcy's part in putting a stop to 'a most imprudent marriage' produces in her later that storm of indignation before which, if he at all bows, Darcy remains undaunted. Yet, despite her reluctance, and her rejoinder that few young people are withheld by lack of adequate means from entering into engagements, she can heed her aunt's advice not to involve herself with Wickham in a match 'which the want of fortune would make so very imprudent'. In instinct Elizabeth is so little inclined to dissent from the prevailing view that, when Lydia announces exultingly that Wickham is 'safe' in having given up Mary King, she can add quietly, 'And Mary King is safe! safe from a connection imprudent as to fortune.' Dog in a manger this might perhaps be, but it is also conviction.

So important is fortune where attachment is concerned that a bidding price normally applies itself to a marriageable young person. Thus Elinor is informed by her brother that the lady intended for Edward Ferrars is the Hon. Miss Morton, only daughter of the late Lord Morton, 'with thirty thousand pounds'; and the story which tells well round Highbury on Mr Elton's return starts with the fact that he 'had not thrown himself away – he had gained a woman of 10,000*l* or thereabouts'. The match between Miss Maria Ward and Sir Thomas Bertram, of Mansfield Park, was something of a nine days' wonder, for her fortune was a mere seven thousand pounds, and even her lawyer uncle judged her to be 'at least three thousand pounds short of any equitable claim to it'. A similar honesty obliges the Reverend and Mrs Richard Morland to concede that 'under every pecuniary view', Catherine's marriage to Henry Tilney would be 'a match beyond the claim of their daughter'. Such is Mr Crawford's offer to Fanny Price; her uncle is roused so far from his customary composure as to tell her that her rejecting a man of so large estate can be the result only of 'a wild fit of folly'.

It must not for a moment be thought that a woman's beauty does not affect the transaction: how can it not have relevance? But an Emma Woodhouse of course is apt to place far too high a value on it. John Dashwood is closer to the spirit of affairs in kindly making known to his elder sister his calculation that Marianne, with her changed looks after illness, would be unlikely to attach a man of more than five or six hundred a year, and confiding that she (Elinor) is now almost certain to do better. Dashwood's besetting tendency to see everything in monetary terms renders him more, not less, of a realist in this regard. Mary Crawford's pragmatic if often cynical common sense expresses as unerringly the outlook of the world which has nurtured her, in inspiring her first reaction to her brother's announcement of his wish to marry Fanny:

> 'Lucky, lucky girl!' cried Mary as soon as she could speak – 'what a match for her! My dearest Henry, this must be my *first* feeling; but my *second*, which you shall have as sincerely, is that I approve your choice from my soul.'

Anne Steele is completely unlike Mary Crawford, being senseless, for a start. But in her function of eavesdropper she is as faithful a spokesman for society in reporting Miss Godby's saying to Miss Sparks 'that nobody in their senses could expect Mr Ferrars to give up a woman like Miss Morton, with thirty thousand pounds to her fortune, for Lucy Steele that had nothing at all'. By those standards, so to act would be folly. When he is prevailed on to authorise something similar in his son's engagement to the poorly dowered Catherine Morland, General Tilney, uniting paternal forbearance with conformity to the outlook of his times, gives Henry permission 'to be a fool if he liked it!'

More than anything else, it is wealth, or the lack of it, which can be seen to determine the state of mind and dictate the actions of marriageable persons in Jane Austen's novels. This is Elinor's own conclusion as she grieves and wonders at Edward Ferrars's depressed spirits, and the inconsistency of his behaviour towards her. She is confident he knows of her regard for him; she tells herself therefore that the root of the trouble is his 'dependent situation', and tries to convince Marianne that it must place many difficulties in his way should he wish to marry a woman who had neither great fortune nor high rank. For precisely the same reason she is ready to understand Willoughby and Marianne's not publishing their engagement. Though knowing him independent, she has heard his estate estimated by Sir John to be no more than six or seven hundred a year; and as he lives at a much higher rate and there is no other indication of riches, she can 'easily conceive that marriage might not be immediately in their power'. Similar reasonings, and the feelings accompanying them, the author herself might have had direct experience of. Her admirer Tom Lefroy, with whom she had flirted quite notably for a year or two, was banished from her presence by his elders on the grounds of being too young and poor to think of marriage.[1]

A prominent theme in her writing is that of young people waiting patiently or despondently for the means of marrying, or concealing their engagement so as not to offend those from whom they have expectations of wealth. Fanny Harville has died at the end of the year or two she and Captain Benwick had been waiting for fortune and promotion. Eleanor Tilney's noble lover has been 'long withheld only by inferiority of situation from addressing her', the difficulty being removed by his 'unexpected accession to title and fortune'. Anne Elliot, having refused Captain Wentworth because of 'the independence which alone had been wanting', has decided that his failure to return to her when he has made his fortune at sea must indicate either his indifference or his unwillingness to hazard another rejection. Even Robert Martin in his state of yeomanly self-sufficiency will not propose to Harriet without proving – to himself and Mr Knightley – 'that he could afford it'.

The alternative, entered into by some, of getting engaged secretly upon the expectation of plenty is fraught with perils. It might involve nothing less than waiting in resigned hope for the death of a relative – which, as Elinor points out somewhat needlessly to Lucy Steele, 'is a melancholy and shocking extremity'. And it is bound to lead to complication in being a defiance of society's rules. Elinor accounts for Willoughby's distressing departure by supposing he does not dare to confess being engaged to a girl of whom his rich relation at Allenham Court will disapprove; but while she will go so far as to think it proper to practise concealment from this lady, she can accept no excuse for her own family's being kept in the dark. Emma Woodhouse is ready to make every allowance for a young man in dependent situation having to consider the spirits, pleasure and temper of those who control the purse-strings – this, out of generous inclination to the unknown and non-appearing Frank Churchill, and an inclination less generous to tease Mr Knightley. But though Churchill's plea of the 'difficulties in the

then state of Enscombe' implicit in the late Mrs Churchill's
attitude after receives sympathetic understanding from her, we
hear from Emma when the secret engagement is first revealed
nothing but tones of horror, expressive of the sentiments of
most of those connected with Hartfield, and all in Highbury
unconnected with it, at the 'system of hypocrisy and deceit, –
espionage, and treachery' which has duped them throughout a
whole winter and spring. Churchill's written repentance is
effusive; his fiancée, in few words, confesses her genuine
shame. But they have been impelled to their conduct by the
same force that leads Willoughby to endear himself to Marianne without a thought for her feelings, and then to betray her
despite the pangs inflicted by a first true love. It is the 'dread of
poverty', and the complementary idea – denounced as fraudu-
lent only when he is in possession of them – 'of the necessity of
riches, which I was naturally inclined to feel'. True or false,
they are felt just as naturally and as absolutely, by men and
women alike, in the world that is presented to us.

Most of the heroes of the novels are men of wealth, or at
least of means. Brandon, Darcy, Bingley, Churchill, Knightley
and the latter Captain Wentworth conduct their courtships
unhindered by a money problem. Henry Tilney's determination to marry Catherine despite his father's anger is sustained
by 'a conviction of its justice', but also by a present income of
'independence and comfort' and a certainty of the eventual
reversion of 'a very considerable fortune'. Edward Ferrars
alone is in dire financial straits; and his condemning himself to
live on a mere hundred pounds a year to keep faith with Lucy
when he might have enjoyed an income of over two thousand
by marrying Miss Morton shows an honourable disinterestedness – and an attitude so unusual as to be beyond the comprehension of his brother Robert, who cannot picture to himself a
condition more wretched. Matters are improved by Colonel
Brandon's gift of the Delaford living; but the Colonel must
have shared something of Robert Ferrars's wonderment at
Edward's purposing to take his bride to a rectory which, as he
emphasizes, '*can* do no more than make Mr Ferrars comfortable as a bachelor; it cannot enable him to marry'. It is thus
with almost unexampled fortitude that Edward and Elinor at

length undertake matrimony upon a pittance of eight hundred a year, and in a hovel containing only five sitting rooms on the ground floor and bedroom accommodation for fifteen.

Edward Ferrars would seem to be exemplary in not being driven to the expedient generally resorted to by the impoverished male: marriage to a rich woman. Of course he is not heavily in debt, like the high-living Willoughby, who has looked upon it as a matter of course, as he tells Elinor, that he should 're-establish' his circumstances by marrying a woman of fortune. He has more claim to sympathy than Elizabeth Bennet's first admirer. It is through unvarnished venality rather than a desire to defend a lifestyle that George Wickham planned to elope with the fifteen-year-old Georgiana Darcy, and gain a fortune of thirty thousand pounds thereby. His running off with Lydia Bennet is intended to be an escapade and no more, for she is not rich. When Darcy, having traced them to London, asks him why he had not immediately married Lydia and benefited by the financial help Mr Bennet would have been able to give, he learns, according to Mrs Gardiner, that Wickham 'still cherished the hope of more effectually making his fortune by marriage'.

Such conduct is cold-hearted enough; but can the hope in itself be reprehensible when it is seen to be so widely indulged in, and to be hallowed by lordly precedent? As Colonel Fitzwilliam gives Elizabeth to understand, the younger sons of an earl cannot marry where they like; and, prompted by her retort of, 'Unless where they like women of fortune, which I think they very often do', he admits with more delicacy than daring to there being few in his rank of life who can afford to marry 'without some attention to money'. Is not this also the situation of the heir of a bankrupt baronet? The mystery of young Mr William Walter Elliot's past drawing back from acquaintance with Sir Walter Elliot and his daughter Elizabeth is explained to Anne by her schoolfriend Mrs Smith. At that period of his life, she avers, his one object was to make his fortune – not through his profession of the law, but by marriage. The woman he chose was daughter to a grazier, and granddaughter of a butcher; but though his friends might object to her low birth, he dismissed the thought in the process of using every means to ascertain the real amount of her fortune, before committing himself. 'Money, money, was all that he wanted,' Mrs Smith concludes. By Fitzwilliam's example this conduct is at least prudential; and, indeed, by general allowance it was but natural. Emma Woodhouse, struck by Jane Fairfax's caution and reticence in speaking of the Dixons, especially of his character and of the suitability of the match, deduces there and then that Mr Dixon had perhaps had an affectionate regard for her while courting his future wife, 'or had been fixed only to Miss Campbell, for the sake of the future twelve thousand pounds'.

In this climate of thought – and practice – are we to despise John Thorpe when, having brought to an end the praise of his own horsemanship for his fair passenger's benefit, he questions Catherine on 'old Allen's' wealth and childless condition, and comments in artless style and with evident design, 'A famous thing for his next heirs. He is *your* godfather, is not he?' Is not Thorpe doing as any other young man in his position would do? Apart from instances the novels themselves supply, we have the testimony of two worldly-wise observers. The first is Mrs Smith, who, intent on making Anne acquainted with the black-heartedness of Mr Elliot, hesitates a little when Anne presumes it was his marrying for money which first opened her friend's eyes to his character. 'Oh!' she replies, 'those things are too common. When one lives in the world, a man or woman's marrying for money is too common to strike one as it ought.' She had seen, at that time, nothing reprehensible in Elliot's doing ' "the best for himself" '; it had indeed 'passed as a duty'. The other witness is none other than Mrs Jennings, a shade less grammatical, but if anything more shrewdly perceptive. At the revelation of Willoughby's perfidy she is torn between two positions, born respectively of emotion and better knowledge. She finds it the oddest thing, she tells Elinor, that a young man should so treat a pretty girl; 'But when there is plenty of money on one side, and next to none on the other, Lord bless you! they care no more about such things!

–' Soon returning to the other side of the matter on the impulse of pity, she argues with herself, 'Why don't he, in such a case, sell his horses, let his house, turn off his servants, and make a thorough reform at once?' Rhetoric, as ever though, will not avail against reality, and she answers her own question: 'But that won't do now-a-days; nothing in the way of pleasure can ever be given up by the young men of this age.'

The only thing wrong with Mrs Jennings's reasoning, apart from ambiguity, is its failure to take the young women into account. They are inclined to be just as mercenary – if such a thing may be said – as the young men. Mrs Jennings's friend and crony Sir John Middleton, for all his gallantry to attractive girls, is here under no illusion. Elinor has no sooner asked who Willoughby is and where he lives than he is laughingly assuring her, 'Yes, yes, he is well worth catching, I can tell you, Miss Dashwood.' In so doing he earns the rebuke of Mrs Dashwood, who has suffered an earlier affront of the same nature in the shape of a warning from her daughter-in-law of the danger which would attend any young woman – meaning Elinor – who attempted to '*draw in*' her brother Edward Ferrars with an eye to his expectations. When we bear in mind how Caroline Bingley, who has no less than twenty thousand pounds to her name, endeavours to *draw in* Mr Darcy, we will be inclined to forgive Isabella Thorpe her grave looks as she pronounces 'charming' the modest settlement which the Reverend Richard Morland proposes. Little surprise is invited by her leaving James for Captain Tilney – to whom, according to his brother Henry, she will just as predictably be constant 'unless a baronet should come in her way'.

Isabella is very different from her friend; yet are we to say that Catherine Morland, the most genuine of heroines, has no fiscal consideration in mind when, having elicited from Mrs Allen all the information Mrs Hughes has given her about the Tilneys, she concludes with the salient question, 'And is Mr Tilney, my partner, the only son?' Her inquiry is in the circumstances of the times natural, even laudable; it reveals her as more than a mere girl. And it is with motive as befitting that Charlotte Lucas urges Elizabeth, for whose hand Darcy has just asked at the Netherfield ball, not to play the simpleton and allow her fancy for Wickham to make her unattractive in the eyes of a man of ten times his consequence. The plea is yielded to for reasons of decorum more than anything else. Elizabeth will not respond with the singleness of mind a Mary Crawford displays at her 'warm-hearted, unreserved' stepsister's plan, communicated the moment she enters the house, for an alliance between her twenty thousand pounds and the status of baronet's heir enjoyed by Tom Bertram. Mary, as she immediately afterwards apprises Dr Grant, is no enemy to matrimony; everyone, she feels, ought to marry as soon as they can do so 'to advantage'; and she is soon giving thought to Mrs Grant's proposition according to the measure of due priorities. The park, the house, the furniture, the sisters and the mother having all found favour, Tom Bertram is adjudged 'an agreeable man himself'.

Such sentiments as these are clearly to be seen as indelicate, perhaps indicative of the 'corrupted' mind the shocked Edmund later apprehends. But the philosophy underlying them, which Mary is to express with frankness in the precept, 'A large income is the best recipé for happiness I ever heard of', is far too much part of the common mentality to be treated with contempt. Indeed, its prominence in the mind of Miss Maria Bertram might lead us to wonder as to the outlook of the generality of well-meaning young women of lesser rank and fortune. Maria having begun at the age of twenty-one to think of matrimony as a duty, and perceived that marriage to Mr Rushworth, for whom she had neither affection nor regard, will give her

> the enjoyment of a larger income than her father's, as well as ensure her the house in town, which was now a prime object, it became, by the same rule of moral obligation, her evident duty to marry Mr Rushworth if she could.

The position is bluntly, if not crudely, stated. We may if we wish react in the manner of Elizabeth Bennet (who is by way of being a radical for her times, and also something of a purist) and account the behaviour of Mary Crawford and Maria

Bertram a forsaking of 'principle and integrity'; but we might otherwise see these girls as possessing an in-built seniority of disposition. For if the equating of wealth with happiness is rife amongst the young, it is more so amongst their elders. The implications of filial duty are conveyed with gentleness in Mrs Gardiner's warning to Elizabeth about the impecunious Wickham, and somewhat less mildly in the conduct of General Tilney. Henry and Eleanor can only look at each other as Catherine ingenuously affirms that Isabella's interests are sure to be safe with a future father-in-law who, professedly, values money only as it allows him to promote his children's happiness. They are already in a state of astonishment at the General's flattering attentions to Catherine when there is clearly 'nothing in her situation likely to engage their father's particular respect'. His wrath on discovering that she is not an heiress has at least the merit of reassuring them as to his consistency. While under illusion he had been making it perfectly evident to Henry where his duty lay; and his offensive launched against Catherine is the continuation of his economic diplomacy by other means.

Far more usual, without doubt, is the action of Colonel Brandon's father in cynically marrying off his ward to his eldest son, who does not love her, simply because 'Her fortune was large, and our family estate much encumbered'. The prevalence of this sort of calculation, and use of authority, explains Anne Elliot's dwelling with such warmth on the Musgroves' treatment of Charles Hayter and Henrietta. 'What a blessing for young people to be in such hands!' she exclaims to Charles. 'Your father and mother seem so totally free from all those ambitious feelings which have led to so much misconduct and misery, both in young and old!' Charles's earlier mentioning that Mr Musgrove 'would be as well pleased if the gentleman were richer' is calculated to keep the reader's feet firmly on the ground. That Anne is thinking in general terms, and not specially of the erstwhile behaviour of her own father, is borne out by the way Sir Thomas Bertram views Maria's engagement to Mr Rushworth. The alliance is 'exactly of the right sort', materially and politically, one which it would have pained him to relinquish; and his happiness at the prospect of so great an increase of 'respectability and influence' compels him 'to think any thing of his daughter's disposition that was most favourable for the purpose'. Only later does it dawn on him that, knowing the young lady's true feelings, he has sacrificed the right to the expedient, and been urged on by selfish and materialistic motives. By the stage where he gives a joyful consent to Edmund's marrying Fanny he is said to be 'Sick of ambitious and mercenary connections', prizing by contrast 'the sterling good of principle and temper'. This discovery, most in his position have yet to make. That 'not one speculative thought' of Willoughby's becoming her son-in-law has been raised in the mind of Mrs Dashwood by his prospect of riches is a fact which marks her as both singular and admirable.

Parental pressure to marry for money is quite the usual thing. It is not always as spectacular in operation as it proves itself in events at Northanger Abbey, or in Harley-street, where Fanny Dashwood's hysterics at the revelation of her elder brother's engagement to Lucy Steele, interrupted only to order the Miss Steeles instantly out of the house, continue throughout the long day. Edward's disregarding of 'Duty, affection, every thing' in persisting despite his mother's wishes, and Mrs Ferrars's consigning him to penury if not perdition with the superadded vow of obstructing his advancement in any profession he might enter, we learn of only from John Dashwood's report. But society's way of dealing with man or woman who defies duty to finance and family is decisive. The Miss Churchill of Enscombe who marries Captain Weston is thrown off 'with due decorum' by her proud and offended parents; and the Miss Frances Ward who, favouring a Lieutenant of Marines, marries 'to disoblige her family', in the common phrase, receives the same treatment from her titled sister. Not that unpleasantness was intended: it was Mrs Norris who wrote the angry letter. Lady Bertram, in her tranquillity and indolence of disposition, would, we are told, have contented herself with merely giving up her sister, and thinking no more of the matter. With Octavius Caesar, she is inclined to 'let determin'd things to destiny/Hold unbewail'd their way'.

In the ninth year of Fanny's acquaintance with her, Lady Bertram is roused to some semblance of activity and unselfishness by the news of Henry Crawford's proposal. 'It is every young woman's duty to accept such a very unexceptionable offer as this,' she declares. By this first piece of advice she has ever received from her aunt, Fanny is silenced – if not by Lady Bertram's heroic readiness to do without her if she were married to 'a man of such good estate as Mr Crawford'. The laws of love forbid Fanny's acquiescence; but the theme of duty to property and position is one which speaks movingly to the hearts of old and young. Despite her certainty that she and Mr Elliot are incompatible, Anne Elliot is 'obliged to turn away, to rise, to walk to a distant table, and, leaning there in pretended employment, try to subdue the feelings' created by the picture of herself as future mistress of Kellynch Hall that her friend Lady Russell places before her. Similarly, Emma Woodhouse, strolling in maiden meditation through the Donwell Abbey grounds, feels 'all the honest pride and complacency' of family alliance as she views the imposing size and style of the building in its pleasant situation, and becomes sensible of 'an increasing respect for it' as the residence of a family of true gentility.

These are emotions indeed. Whether or not Charlotte Brontë's charge that Jane Austen knows nothing of the passions and gives only distant recognition to the feelings is true of her treatment of sexual love, it does not hold good upon the subject of possessions. Here, if at all, are to be detected the true and unmistakable stirrings of emotion. In Maria Bertram the manifestation, not surprisingly, is potent. Earlier, her cool indifference to her lover could not have been made more obvious; but as the coach party approaches Sotherton she is unable to observe casually that she believes it is now ' "all Mr Rushworth's property on each side of the road," without elation of heart'.

The episode cannot but remind us of the more famous surveying of property that takes place in Derbyshire. To what extent Elizabeth Bennet's ardour is aroused or enhanced by the sight of Pemberley House is not immediately apparent. Her impression that to be its mistress 'might be something!' occurs fittingly as the prospect of the building in its enchanting setting first greets the eyes of the travellers when their carriage clears the wood and reaches the top of an eminence. And the threatening sensation of 'something like regret' which tempers her thoughts as she passes through the rooms, and provokes the reflection, 'And of this place I might have been mistress!' is just as natural, especially in its being commingled with admiration, and appreciation of good taste. However, though no clue is afforded by particular words and actions, the incident as a whole may possibly provide one. That Elizabeth is impressed by the scale and grandeur of Pemberley is certain; and there is present in her manner, as the vocal Mrs Reynolds takes the party round, a disquiet which lies between restlessness and agitation, and which we have not known in her before. But she is in the home of Mr Darcy, towards whom her feelings have already undergone change through greater knowledge and unforced respect. If, therefore, the 'stateliness of money and rank' does affect her heart at Pemberley – having swayed not at all at Rosings, in her mood of defiance – it would appear to remain Elizabeth's secret. She is a child of her age, though; and if a truth spoken in jest may be conjectured in her telling Jane that the commencement of her love for Darcy dates 'from my first seeing his beautiful grounds at Pemberley', it is to be allowed its full weight.

There are women, as well as men, in the novels with whom wealth is not a prime consideration. Elizabeth may be one. The number includes Mrs Dashwood and Elinor, and the elegant yet reassuringly human Jane Fairfax, for whose disinterestedness Mr Knightley vouches. His wonder, in doing so, that Frank Churchill should be 'Assured of the love of such a woman' implies that such women are few. His friend Mrs Weston, admirable in all other respects, is alas not one of them. Herself of lower status than Jane when she married (Jane never having been a governess), she has adapted so well to her new position as to tell Emma at the first news of her stepson's engagement that they must 'make the best of it', and so incline Mr Weston to be content with the match. 'It is not a connection to gratify,' she states, in the best accents of the society in which she is now established; then adds, with the epitome of its logic, 'but if Mr Churchill does not feel that, why should we?'

Jane Fairfax and Elizabeth Bennet are presumably instruments of what Arnold Kettle calls the 'realistic, unromantic, and indeed, by orthodox standards, subversive concern with the position of women that gives the tang and force' to the writer's consideration of marriage.[2] The former startles and quite unsettles Mrs Elton – if not the reader – by gruesome mention of the need she will have in her poverty of seeking a livelihood through the assistance of 'Offices for the sale – not quite of human flesh – but of human intellect'. With less bitterness, but greater scorn – and with the same relentless realism – does Elizabeth turn upon Colonel Fitzwilliam, who has decorously hinted at the financial stringencies which inure younger sons to 'self-denial and dependence' and oblige them to court women possessed of wealth: 'And pray, what is the usual price of an Earl's younger son? Unless the elder brother is very sickly, I suppose you would not ask above fifty thousand pounds?' The satirical taunt of a kind of prostitution present in these words is not a degree less than savage. Elizabeth is her father's daughter: this is a 'set down' after his own style, but deadlier. It makes the *coup de grâce* he administers to Mr Collins, advising him to stand by the nephew rather than the aunt because 'He has more to give', seem like a mild reproach.

Elizabeth must be recognised as having a further claim to distinction in the indifference she shows to Darcy's riches during her earlier acquaintance with him. She is perfectly aware of its unusualness, and just as sure of its effect. After they are engaged, and she has mischievously asked him to account for his falling in love with her, she volunteers her own opinion with characteristic candour. 'The fact is,' she declares, 'that you were sick of civility, of deference, of officious attention. You were disgusted with the women who were always speaking and looking, and thinking for *your* approbation alone. I roused, and interested you, because I was so unlike them.' That this remark has substance is evident from the conduct of Caroline Bingley, and Darcy's own contemptuous reference to the 'arts which ladies sometimes condescend to employ for captivation'. But better proof lies in the reaction of Elizabeth's parents to her wanting to marry the man they think she so dislikes. Mr Bennet instantly assumes it is the lure of wealth which, as he states it, makes her 'determined to have him'; and Mrs Bennet's rejoicing that the temptation has been dealt with by being given in to approaches the pitch of ecstasy.

The Bennets are perhaps not an ordinary family, but nothing can redeem the Lucases from the charge. Their behaviour upon Charlotte's engagement may be taken to indicate the norm. 'Joyful alacrity' greets the news. Mr Collins's present circumstances and 'exceedingly fair' prospects of future wealth make it a most eligible match for a girl with little fortune. Lady Lucas is set calculating guilelessly how many more years Mr Bennet's tenure of life is likely to last. The younger girls are gleeful at the chance of coming out earlier; the boys are relieved that their sister will not have to die an old maid – and live a long life presumably supported by them. The question of Mr Collins's character does not appear to have arisen within the family; and by Charlotte herself it has, with studious resolve, been put to one side. She is sure he is neither sensible nor agreeable; she has found his society irksome, and knows his affection for her must be imaginary. But she is aware that marriage is 'the only honourable provision for well-educated young women of small fortune'. However uncertain it is of affording happiness, it must be 'their pleasantest preservative from want'.

Elizabeth Bennet may not be mercenary; and she is with reason dismayed at the indelicacy implicit in marriage entered into as a transaction in the absence of liking. But the logic of Charlotte's position she has no means of refuting in their interview, because it is unanswerable. Her silence is thus doubly discreet when she encounters it once more, this time from the lips of an irate mother.

> 'But I tell you what, Miss Lizzy, if you take it into your head to go on refusing every offer of marriage in this way, you will never get a husband at all – and I am sure I do not know who is to maintain you when your father is dead.'

Elizabeth is not so much 'a thing ensky'd and sainted' as to be insensitive to material advantage – any more than is Emma

Woodhouse, who does not need Mr Knightley to point out to her how important it has been to Miss Taylor, at her time of life, to be secure of a 'comfortable provision'. This kind of thinking, scarcely negligible in the mind of a heroine, is obsessive in Mrs Bennet, for whom the business of life is to get her daughters married. We laugh, with her husband, that her response to a young man of four or five thousand a year coming to the neighbourhood should be, 'What a fine thing for our girls!' – but the author's comment that Mr Bennet was among the earliest of those who waited on Mr Bingley must not escape us. Jane Austen refrains from causing him also to proclaim it 'a delightful thing' to have a daughter well married; but she would be falsifying the nature of her society if she did not make him see it as a subject of great concern and urgency.

The very texture of the language in which the novels are written witnesses to the mercenary aspect of marriage. The persistency with which buried metaphors in Jane Austen's prose reiterate the values of commerce and property, the counting house and the inherited estate, has been demonstrated by Mark Schorer. They relate to scale, in words like high and low, advance and decline; to money, with its vocabulary of credit, value, interest, and so on; to business and property, with terms such as inherit, procure, certify, entitle and scheme; to number and measure, by the common use of ideas relating to addition, division and multiplication; and to matter, in concepts such as weight and substance. This loading of the writer's style creates 'a world of peculiarly *material* value, a world of almost instinctive material interests in its basic, intuitive response to experience'. On the surface of the action, however, is projected a very different world: one of refinement, of sensibility, and of moral concern; and in the tension between the kinds of value, material and moral, is to be found the cause of those discrepancies from which comedy arises. It is in the process of adjustment of the two scales of estimation, and not by a victory of the one over the other, that the heroine's fate is determined. The verbal fabric of the novels thus warns the reader against being enticed by superficial sentiment into ignoring the shaping forces of property and rank which operate in the depths. And it asks him to realise he is reading a story, not of courtship and marriage, but about 'the economic and social significance of courtship and marriage': for in each novel it is from the matter of finance that the basic situation originates.[3]

The association of matrimony with the mercenary is insistent, and its influence all-pervasive: the phenomenon forms part of the atmosphere the characters breathe. Contemplated in itself, it would be sordid; W.H. Auden is not alone in evincing shock and discomfort at this matter-of-fact description by a middle-class English spinster of 'the amorous effects of "brass" '.[4] But here Mr Collins must be taken into the reckoning, for he comes to purge away the gloom – and to do so, not as a mere object of merriment, but by bringing upon the scene in his own person a modicum of purity. From the first we hear the strain of a higher mood in his concern at being the means of injuring the amiable Miss Bennets as future possessor of the Longbourn estate, and his readiness to make the girls amends, though these introductory notes do strike discordantly upon the ears of most of the Bennet family. Elizabeth dismisses his apology for being next in the entail: 'We cannot suppose he would help it, if he could,' she observes with robust scepticism. But Jane, while puzzled as to what the atonement might be, sees the wish itself as 'certainly to his credit'; and so might we, for we are in the presence of other than financial motivation. Mr Collins himself has no doubt of the meritoriousness of his plan to choose a wife from among the Bennet girls and thus minimise their pecuniary loss upon their father's death; he views it as 'excessively generous and disinterested', and is sure it will be found so by Elizabeth as, in the course of proposing to her, he professes perfect indifference to considerations of fortune. True, he will not refuse the one thousand pounds in the 4 per cents. he knows will be her modest ultimate entitlement; and his making no further demand on Mr Bennet is inspired by the very good reason that there will be no more to be had. But at least he is not marrying for money; and in the prevailing climate of thought, is not this attitude a veritable blast of fresh air?

The cynic might hold that it is not altruism but realism: Mr Collins knows his unattractiveness to women, and thus will not hold out for financial gain in the business of attachment. But so to believe would be to do injustice to his vanity. If, as the author tells us, he 'thought too well of himself to comprehend on what motive his cousin could refuse him', his expectation of other women would be no whit dissimilar.

But having no monetary incentive oneself does not imply blindness to such motivation in others. On the contrary, it is because he is aware of its almost invariable presence that Mr Collins is moved to look on the rejection of his addresses as 'merely words of course'. He supplies his reasons for this belief as readily as he has favoured Elizabeth with those for his wanting to marry. 'It does not appear to me that my hand is unworthy of your acceptance, or that the establishment I can offer would be any other than highly desirable.' How seemly this explicitness is, and what needful sentiments find no place in his thinking, are matters also to be brought into an assessment. However, in the context of a materialistic society in which marriage is universally viewed in terms of wealth and possessions, Mr Collins is speaking powerful and moving fact.

But is it not also insulting fact? Does it not embolden him, in a manner as insufferable as it is absurd, to inform Elizabeth that the effects of her beauty and 'amiable qualifications' will be so overshadowed by her poverty that no one is likely to want to marry her, and on these grounds to presume to doubt her sincerity? Is it even believable that a young woman should be treated in this way? The answer is in the affirmative. Much the same assurance, importing the same style of compliment, is bestowed on his sister Elinor by John Dashwood – though it is to exertion, not to resignation, that he summons her. Colonel Brandon, he is convinced, has a liking for her, but the issue is in doubt: 'Perhaps just at present he is undecided; the smallness of your fortune may make him hang back; his friends may all advise against it.' The Colonel is therefore to be enticed by those feminine wiles which can 'fix him, in spite of himself'. As for any disabling notion she might still retain concerning Edward Ferrars, her poverty renders the chance of being addressed by him 'quite out of the question, the objections are insurmountable – you have too much sense not to see all that'. To these pleasant confidences, as to the intimation that his wife and mother-in-law are anxious to see her well settled, Elinor, we are informed, will vouchsafe no answer.

John Dashwood is not the most estimable of men; but this cannot be said of George Knightley, who, with equal frankness and lack of ceremony, derides another young lady's prospects – not to her face, but to her friend's face. The lady is Harriet Smith, upon whose beauty, sweetness of disposition and manner, and modesty, Emma has been energetically dwelling as 'the highest claims a woman could possess'. Knightley brusquely rejoins that Emma is abusing her reason. 'Better be without sense,' he declares, 'than misapply it as you do.' Mr Elton, if she is thinking of him as a husband for Harriet, 'knows the value of a good income as well as anybody,' may talk sentimentally but will act rationally, and is acquainted with a bevy of young ladies with twenty thousand pounds apiece. Though the hurt in this case is only to Emma's feelings, the reasoning is identical to that of Mr Collins.

And might not that disregard for a woman which may be induced by the crass weight of possessions take on a more insidious form, in the very midst of real attachment and devotion? Darcy, in proposing to Elizabeth Bennet, speaks of his apprehension and misery; 'but his countenance', she notes, 'expressed real security.' If this confidence is not due to anything she has said or done, might it not stem in part from the fact of his immense wealth? However this may be, the effect on Elizabeth is not to be ignored: 'Such a circumstance could only exasperate farther.' It cannot have caused pleasure when Mr Collins was the suitor.

From the start, Mr Collins has shown himself keenly conscious of the importance of the financial aspect of matrimony. His first words relate to the handsomeness of the Bennet girls and his confidence that they would in due time be well disposed of in marriage. If the sentiment is scarcely to the girls' taste, the comment itself is quite in keeping with attitudes generally taken: though it might be hateful in its grossness, the essential truth is not open to question. But no such excuse, it might be thought, can apply to the crowning absurdity in Mr

Collins's amatory advances: his promising Elizabeth that he will be 'uniformly silent' about the smallness of her dowry, no 'ungenerous reproach' ever passing his lips. We find the idea comical, and perfectly ludicrous as part of a proposal. Without doubt it is; yet we should do well in this respect not to ignore the observations by which Elinor Dashwood tries to cure her sister's romantic regard for the now-married Willoughby.

Had they married, she tells Marianne, they must always have been poor. His spendthrift and self-indulgent nature allied to her inexperience would have involved them, despite all attempts at economy, in grievous distresses.

> 'Beyond *that*, had you endeavoured, however reasonably, to abridge *his* enjoyments, is it not to be feared, that instead of prevailing on feelings so selfish to consent to it, you would have lessened your own influence on his heart, and made him regret the connection which had involved him in such difficulties?'

The word reproach is not used by Elinor; but it does not need to be. Whatever may be his failings, Mr Collins, seeing marriage for what it is in the novels' world, is no less realistic in being aware of the dissonances which may mar relationships in an 'imprudent' match. And what he lacks in romantic delicacy upon the subject he more than makes up for by his own lack of mercenary motivation.

5

Station

Any acclaim Mr Collins might gain on the swings of matrimony he is in danger of losing on the roundabouts of rank. For, without social standing himself, he displays undiscriminating respect for degree and those who possess it. While we assume that the truly superior will, as always, desire to wear their formal distinction lightly, we find Mr Collins exulting in the system, for all the world like the valet of any new-made lord taking delight in his master's place in society – or like the master himself, should he be the vain and arrogant Sir Walter Elliot. His zeal for the state of inglorious vassalage is, we must think, simply and unquestionably comic.

What degree of assent Jane Austen might herself have given to the doctrine, penned by Robert Burns near the turn of the century, that

> The rank is but the guinea's stamp;
> The man's the gowd for a' that!

would be an interesting speculation. The certainty is that she endows her characters with the attitudes in this regard she has encountered in real life. They tend to be curiously unenlightened.

Thus Sir Thomas Bertram's chief concern, when it is proposed he should receive Fanny into his house, is for the proper preservation of rank. Unwilling to countenance the smallest measure of despite in his children towards the newcomer, he must still inculcate the truth that they 'cannot be equals'; and without depressing Fanny's spirits too far, he must provide cause for her to remember that she is not a Miss Bertram. The matter he confesses to be one of great delicacy, and he welcomes Mrs Norris's help in determining 'exactly the right line of conduct'; he can find nothing ominous in the lady's remarking that she dare say Fanny would not grow up so handsome as her cousins. The nature of Mrs Norris's discretion is never in doubt, from the moment of her advising the Bertram girls of its being undesirable that Fanny should equal them in accomplishment, to the irate accusation in front of the cast of *Lovers' Vows* that Fanny is 'very ungrateful indeed, considering who and what she is', for her shrinking refusal to take part in the play. But if Mrs Norris errs on the side of degree – to the extent of inducing an admission from Sir Thomas, on his finding the young woman desired by the wealthy Mr Crawford sitting in her room on a cold day without the benefit of a fire, 'that there has been sometimes, in some points, a misplaced distinction' – she has at least played safe. That in an issue of this kind it is better to do so than be sorry is Edmund Bertram's theme at the prospect of Charles Maddox taking the part of Anhalt consequent upon his own declining to do so. According to Tom Bertram, Maddox is 'as gentlemanlike a man as you will see any where', and will not disgrace them; but the very idea strikes his brother with horror.

> 'This is the end of all the privacy and propriety which was talked about at first. I know no harm of Charles Maddox; but the excessive intimacy which must spring from his being admitted among us in this manner, is highly objectionable, the *more* than intimacy – the familiarity. I cannot think of it with any patience – and it does appear to me an evil of such magnitude as must, *if possible*, be prevented.'

Only where his ultimate dealings with Miss Mary Crawford are concerned is there to be found in the humane Edmund such degree of discomposure as he exhibits when the shades of Mansfield Park are thus threatened with pollution.

It is from this condition of dreadful disrepute that Emma Woodhouse is intent on saving the fair Harriet, by the process of detaching her from bad acquaintance and introducing her into good society. Fearing that the girl will 'sink herself for ever' if she is not taken care of, Emma urges her to fight for social distinction in being supposedly a gentleman's daughter. 'You must support your claim to that station by every thing within your own power,' she asserts, 'or there will be plenty of people who would take pleasure in degrading you.' Emma is using the strongest terms, and the question of course is whether she is exaggerating the whole thing in order to indulge her own snobbery in conjunction with a lust for power. This seems to be the case when she contrives to detect awkward looks, an abrupt manner and an uncouth voice in the excellent Robert Martin. But Harriet is least indecisive where her social advancement is at issue: erratic in judgment and beset with vagaries though she be, the subject makes good sense to her. Upon her first visit to Hartfield she is delighted with Miss Woodhouse's 'affability' and actually shaking hands with her; and at the thought of being excluded from Emma's company through an unacceptable marriage she is aghast. Is it solely affection for her patroness, or the admixture of fear of social debasement, which makes her cry, 'Dear me! – how should I ever have borne it? It would have killed me never to come to Hartfield any more!'? The substantiality of rank she would seem, in her way, to be as convinced of as is Emma herself.

If Emma's ideas are wrong, they are honestly held. Only loyalty to her young friend can blind her to the fact pointed out by Mr Knightley that men of any pretension would shun a girl of Harriet's obscurity; she herself flinches before 'the horror of being in danger of falling in with the second rate and third rate of Highbury', even for the few hours' duration of the Coles' dinner party. It is her conscious wish to make them understand, by declining their invitation, that it was not for them to arrange the terms on which the superior families should visit them. As for being proposed to by Mr Elton, it is an insult and no less: for 'he must know that in fortune and consequence she was greatly his superior.' Intimations of another order do come to trouble her. Though she counts it folly to be disturbed by it in view of the evils of the connection, she finds the conduct of Elizabeth and Robert Martin toward Harriet at Ford's to be distinguished by real feeling; and she tells herself after taking her friend to visit at Abbey-Mill Farm for the regulation fifteen minutes that she would have given or endured a great deal 'to have had the Martins in a higher rank of life'. But the mood cannot last: the main facts reassert themselves. At Donwell Abbey she indulges in the pleasant reflections arising from realisation that Isabella, in marrying John Knightley, 'had given them neither men, nor names, nor places, that could raise a blush'. There she encounters Mrs Elton, whom she has derided as bringing her husband 'no name, no blood, no alliance', being the daughter of a Bristol shopkeeper and niece of an uncle in the law line. It is small wonder, therefore, that the penultimate possibility of Harriet's marrying George Knightley – to whom she has said, 'Were you, yourself, ever to marry, she is the very woman for you' – induces in Emma an extreme of perturbation grounded (as she apprehends it) upon the affront to rank:

> Such an elevation on her side! Such a debasement on his! – It was horrible to Emma to think how it must sink him in the general opinion, to foresee the smiles, the sneers, the merriment it would prompt at his expense.

The personal cause she has to dread that event does not, we may think, too much colour her impression of how society would react to it.

By the end, Emma has sufficiently relaxed her prejudices to be able to look forward with pleasure to meeting Robert Martin. But her subversive whim of trying to propel obscure young women into impossible distinction will be cured by her own experience, if not by Mr Knightley's tutelage. One must doubt the extent to which even a Highbury leopard can change its spots. Emma's thinking has throughout been like that of Mr Bingley's sisters – who, undeterred by their own fortunes having been acquired by trade, look scornfully upon girls whose uncles are a tradesman and a former lawyer's clerk. The mention of Elizabeth's 'fine eyes' leads Mrs Hurst to profess an excessive regard for Jane Bennet, but a fear that with such low connections there is no chance of her being well settled. Her view is confirmed by Mr Darcy himself, who confutes Bingley's warm objection that a Cheapside populated with uncles would not make the Bennet sisters one jot less agreeable, with the chilling and unanswerable comment that 'it must very materially lessen their chance of marrying men of any consideration in the world'.

Elizabeth's appreciation of the barriers of rank is no less acute than Darcy's. She smiles to herself when he asks at Pemberley to be introduced to Mr and Mrs Gardiner, taking them to be people of fashion. As the introduction is made she steals a sly look at him to see how he bears it; she is prepared for the start of surprise, 'and was not without the expectation of his decamping as fast as he could from such disgraceful companions'. Had she not previously told her aunt that, were he ever to come to Gracechurch Street, he would think a month's ablution insufficient to cleanse him from its impurities? She can 'hardly restrain her astonishment from being visible' when Darcy brings his sister to visit them at Lambton on the very morning of her arrival at Pemberley, and thus courts the good opinion of people with whom, a few months before, it would have been 'a disgrace' to associate.

This understanding on Elizabeth's part serves, ironically, to make the more painful Darcy's confession of his difficulties in the course of the memorable proposal at Hunsford Parsonage. The loftiness amounting to disdain expected and indeed requisite in those endowed with fortune and associating with people of rank, she must have become inured to; and she does not deny her friend Charlotte's assertion that a fine young man like Darcy, with family and fortune in his favour, has what amounts to a right to be proud. But Darcy's dwelling – with a warmth deriving from the consequence to which he is doing violence – on the impediments which her social insignificance has created for him arouses her ire. In terms of her reply to Charlotte, his allowable pride does not give him the right to offend hers. But, accused of insulting her by declaring an affection to which his sense of his own interests and even the promptings of personality are opposed, Darcy is inflexible. He will deny neither his helping to part Bingley from Jane nor his rejoicing in this achievement: 'Towards *him*,' he declares, 'I have been kinder than towards myself.' Even Mr Collins could not have spoken with more mortifying frankness. Elizabeth, we are informed, disdains the appearance of noticing the civil reflection; 'but its meaning did not escape, nor was it likely to conciliate her.'

It is with increasing exasperation that Mr Darcy addresses Elizabeth – caused only in part by her angry rejoinders. What provokes him is the apparently wilful blindness to truth and fact in one for whose qualities of mind he has unbounded respect: the fact of birth, rank and wealth, and of the degradation it must constitute for a Darcy to ally himself with the Bennet family. That the scruples he honestly confesses should be in the lady's eyes a cause of offence and not a mark of devotion incenses him. 'They were natural and just,' he cries. 'Could you expect me to rejoice in the inferiority of your connections? To congratulate myself on the hope of relations, whose condition in life is so decidedly beneath my own?' To this question Elizabeth's reply, at that instant, can only be greater anger. But the response which her own thoughts are making to it within a few moments of Darcy's hastily leaving the room shows that, in the stance he has taken and the expectation he has had of her, he has not entirely judged amiss. Of her dislike he has been quite unaware (a circumstance in itself needing to be accounted for), and her charges concerning Jane are unexpected. Both must be injurious to his cause. But the realities of rank and riches and all devolving from them, which he has been so desirous of imparting, do impress themselves. When the hurt to her pride has lessened, realisation that an offer of marriage has been made her despite considerations to whose importance she is no less sensitive than Darcy himself, reduces Elizabeth to wonder. That he should be

> so much in love as to wish to marry her in spite of all the objections which had made him prevent his friend's marrying her sister, and which must appear at least with equal force in his own case, was almost incredible! it was gratifying to have inspired unconsciously so strong an affection.

Truth and fact are often unpalatable. In deciding not to dodge the issue of social distinction, but to speak of it in forthright terms, Darcy may be regarded as acting unwisely and with insensitivity, while deluding himself that he is being creditably frank. He has chosen a line of conduct which is bound to antagonise his beloved. But his action is also an infallible means of demonstrating to her that his affection is real.

In terms of the concepts they present, there is not a great deal to choose between the speeches made to Elizabeth by Darcy and Lady Catherine de Bourgh on the subject of alliance. In both she is reminded that she is a young woman 'without family, connections, or fortune'. Lady Catherine alone credits her with upstart pretensions in her seeming resolve to thwart the union of two affluent houses descended from the same noble line by an intervention repugnant to 'every feeling of propriety and delicacy'. Just as Lady Russell was unprepared for Anne Elliot to be snatched off by a stranger without alliance or fortune, so Lady Catherine cannot be reconciled to her design for her daughter and nephew being frustrated by 'a young woman of inferior birth, of no importance in the world, and wholly unallied to the family!' – particularly since it will be the means by which the son of his late father's steward will be transformed into the nephew's brother-in-law. Her aristocratic being cries out against such unnatural inversion of degree and disruption of order: 'Heaven and earth! – of what are you thinking?' At the hands of his aunt, Elizabeth is insulted and angered – though in a different way – by the same facts of social life as were preached to her by Darcy. Almost as soon, she awakens to their relevance, if not substantiality, and can even expect he will yield to Lady Catherine's persuasions and never renew his proposal. For 'With his notions of dignity, he would probably feel that the arguments, which to Elizabeth had appeared weak and ridiculous, contained much good sense and solid reasoning.'

By this stage, Elizabeth Bennet might be pardonably close to associating the subject of rank with malady and mania; and she would have the further justification that its distinctions are sought the more voraciously the more they are enjoyed, 'As if increase of appetite had grown/By what it fed on.' The predicament in which Sir Walter Elliot finds himself upon his cousin Lady Dalrymple's establishing herself in Laura-place is a corroborative symptom. His rapture, and that of Elizabeth, at such near proximity to bliss is astonishing to Anne in the light

of their exalted ideas of their own station, and she is reduced to
the bizarre wish that they had more pride; and when their
agonising over how to introduce themselves properly is put an
end to by a fulsome and abject letter and the receipt of three
lines of scrawl, her state is one of pure shame. But Lady Russell
approves what has been done, on the principle that 'Family
connections were always worth preserving, good company
always worth seeking'. And Mr Elliot gently reproves Anne for
confusing good company with the best, in her social ideal of
clever, well-informed people who have a great deal of conversation. Good company, he affirms, requires only 'birth,
education and manners, and with regard to education is not
very nice'; and he pronounces it wisdom to enjoy the social
advantages consequent upon reputable kinship.

> 'You may depend upon it, that they will move in the first set in
> Bath this winter, and as rank is rank, your being known to be
> related to them will have its use in fixing your family (our family
> let me say) in that degree of consideration which we must all
> wish for.'

Anne is not convinced. She sees with pain – and not, one
suspects, without suppressed amusement – Sir Walter and
Elizabeth step forward in the Octagon Room to greet their
noble cousin 'with all the eagerness compatible with anxious
elegance', and from thence proceed into the concert room to
draw as many eyes, excite as many whispers, and disturb as
many people as they can in their quest for consequence. But in
these feelings she is isolated. For almost all around her, rank is
rank, and constrains accordingly. Her sister Mary, in being
invited to Camden-place to meet Mr Elliot and be introduced
to Lady Dalrymple and Miss Carteret, 'could not have received a more gratifying attention'. Such is the way of those
born to social eminence; and the boast of the less fortunate
who aspire towards it will similarly comprehend the range of
Mrs Elton's categories of 'Delightful, charming, superior, first
circles, spheres, lines, ranks, every thing'.

Amongst the latter persons, naturally, is Mr Collins. In the
midst of asking Elizabeth to marry him, he protests that he
does not reckon the notice of Lady Catherine de Bourgh as

among the least of the advantages in his power to offer. The silent respect due to rank will, he is confident, acceptably temper the wit and vivacity of his chosen one. When Elizabeth later visits Charlotte at Hunsford, he does not fail to point out afresh his being able to introduce her to very superior society; the exalted theme of 'our intimacy at Rosings' comes near to robbing him of words, and obliges him to walk about the room to allay his emotions. But, if he feels the matter a trifle strongly, his conviction that enjoying the favour of the noble family of de Bourgh is an 'extraordinary advantage and blessing' is one which, in principle, people as diverse as Sir Thomas Bertram, Emma Woodhouse, Fitzwilliam Darcy, Lady Russell and both generations of Walter Elliots could not but approve. They might, though, shrug the shoulder at the way in which their view is borne out by ordinary mortals like Sir William Lucas and Maria in storing the memory with anecdotes and noble names, and the number of times they have been to Rosings.

Might it not be objected that what makes Mr Collins ridiculous is not his conforming to social convention, but the abject way in which he does it? To be set on conducting oneself with grateful respect towards a patron is one thing, but to tell the whole world about it is quite another. Such conscious parading is an extreme of behaviour which must surely be laughable, whatever the subject calling it forth. This one, we learn, elevates Mr Collins to more than usual solemnity of manner; something beyond adulation is at work when he proclaims 'with a most important aspect' Lady Catherine's unexampled condescension, or promises Elizabeth that she will find her politeness beyond anything he can describe. His own comportment in her presence amounts to grovelling: over quadrille at Rosings, apart from giving rapt attention to her anecdotes of herself, he does nothing but agree to her assertions of the mistakes of the three others, thank her for every fish he wins, and apologise if he thinks he wins too many. Anything having reference to her receives from him exaggerated praise. Her house, needless to say, is beyond compare; her opinions on small matters or great have for him the authority of Holy Writ, and are as religiously acquiesced in; and a person 'honoured with some portion of her notice' is but a step away from the vision beatific.

To suggest, even for a moment, a slight similarity in their attitude to greatness between Mr Collins and Mr Bennet might be thought wildly absurd. Yet there is at least a verbal parallel in the former's assuring Elizabeth that Lady Catherine is 'the sort of woman whom one cannot regard with too much deference', and what her father says to her in somewhat shamefast jest concerning Darcy's request for her hand in marriage. 'Lizzy,' he tells her, 'I have given him my consent. He is the sort of man, indeed, to whom I should never dare refuse any thing, which he condescended to ask.' Darcy, whatever his conduct, has in fact never been in danger of the 'set down' for which Mrs Bennet called, and which is finally bestowed on Mr Collins. Of course Mr Bennet will be guilty of none of those excesses of ingratiation which make Mr Collins worthy of the gesture. Unlike his witless wife, however, he will shrink from offending someone of Darcy's eminence; and who is to say that a politic respectfulness is not a form – perhaps one of the higher forms – of flattery?

Flattery, as the standard means of courting the good graces of the powerful, inevitably finds its place in Jane Austen's novels. We may think it a pity; but unless we are prepared to proscribe the desire for social betterment as unworthy of human beings, we must allow flattery to be the perfect means to an end. It is employed by high and low alike, as assiduously by Mrs Norris upon Sir Thomas Bertram and Sir Walter Elliot upon Lady Dalrymple as by Mrs Clay upon Sir Walter and Lucy Steele upon Lady Middleton. Mr Collins is a notable practitioner of the gentle craft; and Lucy, in her triumphs within three families of consequence, may be regarded as a female and more astute Mr Collins. Her delight over the Middletons' furniture and doting fondness for their children captures Lady Middleton's good opinion before she has been an hour at Barton Park; and against the flattery which has subdued her pride, even the close heart of Mrs John Dashwood and the stubborn spirit of Mrs Ferrars have no defence. The method is almost incredibly simple: it is to admire – to admire things and persons with fervour and to the point of obsession, while entertaining no fear of killing the word charming by overwork. We are inclined merely to hold Lucy and her sister in contempt; but we should do well to reflect upon the response of Elinor Dashwood, who, seeing how devotedly they make themselves agreeable to Lady Middleton, 'soon allowed them credit for some kind of sense'.

Perhaps Lucy's greater success is due to her being more selective in her attentions and thus better able to adopt the military strategy of concentrating one's forces. Mr Collins's way, though just as purposeful, is a little more generous: he will heap flatteries upon anyone at all. By inclination and calling, he assures the mystified Darcy at the Netherfield ball, he makes it his object to direct 'attentive and conciliatory manners towards every body', though particularly to his patrons. It is predictable that the weary Netherfield party at the end of the ball will find no refuge from his compliments on the elegance, generosity and politeness of the proceedings. But tribute just as lavish is paid to the vulgar Mrs Philips – than whom, he protests to Mr Bennet after his first visit, with the exception of Lady Catherine and her daughter, he has never seen a more elegant woman: for she most civilly received him, and invited him for a game of lottery tickets and 'a little bit of hot supper' the next evening; and he has never met with so much attention in the whole course of his life. Indeed, in pursuance of his policy he can even approach flattery of his dead father's feelings: he has delayed his reconciliatory overture to the Longbourn family, he tells Mr Bennet in his letter, 'fearing lest it might seem disrespectful to his memory for me to be on good terms with any one, with whom it had always pleased him to be at variance'.

Mr Collins and those of his kidney are consistently and relentlessly pursuing a single aim: to establish themselves in the good opinion of others. They do it through a means as effective as it is crude, and show in the process a knowledge of human nature denied to better, and to more honourable, heads. For they have unfailing insight into man's weakness, which they exploit far more advantageously than if they had looked to his strengths. Jerome K. Jerome has said, unforgettably, that we differ widely in our nobler qualities, and tend to separation in exercising them, but that in vanity and kindred feelings we are at one, and can all join hands:

> Ay, ay, vanity is truly the motive-power that moves Humanity, and it is flattery that greases the wheels. If you want to win affection and respect in this world, you must flatter people. Flatter high and low, rich and poor, and silly and wise. You will get on famously. Praise this man's virtues and that man's vices. Compliment everybody upon everything, and especially upon what they haven't got. Admire guys for their beauty, fools for their wit, and boors for their breeding. Your discernment and intelligence will be extolled to the skies.[1]

What is insidious in Mr Collins is that, vain himself, he is responsive to the vanity of all around him, making it the medium and means of his socialising and advancement. He operates at the level which we pride ourselves on having left behind, but where we are in fact just as vulnerable as those who succumb to his blandishments. In reality, we draw upon our self-contempt in deriding him, sensing, with an instinctive recognition, that our own shame is written into his progress.

6

Colloquy

When Charlotte waylays Mr Collins in the lane by Lucas Lodge, she is agreeably surprised by the amount of love and eloquence which awaits her there. Everything is settled between them in as short a time as his long speeches will permit. One assumes long-windedness, which is tiresome on any occasion, to be specially inopportune in a proposal of marriage; but Mr Darcy is scarcely brief as he sets about making his own declaration. Elizabeth goes through a variety of emotions while he is speaking, and upon anger supervening tries to 'compose herself to answer him with patience, when he should have done'. He seems to take a fair time.

If there was ever an excuse for prolixity, it belongs to the world of formal manners and ostentatious display which Jane Austen knew. For hers was an age of society's predominance, when man was viewed primarily as a social creature, and individuals were to be assessed in relation to their fellows, and according to widely accepted notions of decorum. Conversation being an acknowledged art, the judging of a person from the quality of his talk was if anything more pertinent then than it is today. And the speeches of someone like Mr Collins may be better appreciated in the light of other characteristic utterances.

Human nature not having changed, there can be no surprise that vanity is the chief motive in much of what is spoken. The choice examples in this respect are provided by Robert Ferrars, whose conversation is simply a series of harangues upon his own ability, knowledge and good taste. To impress Elinor Dashwood with his excessive fondness for a cottage as a residence, he tells her how he threw on the fire three plans of Bonomi which Lord Cartland had brought to show him, in the act of advising that peer that a cottage was the thing; or how the distraught Lady Elliot implored him to tell her how a dance could be managed in such confined space, failing to discern what was immediately obvious to him. The vaunt direct, in his hands, becomes a vehicle of detraction. Having been diverted beyond measure by the thought of his brother Edward living as an impecunious clergyman in a cramped parsonage, he turns more seriously to causes. 'Poor Edward! – His manners are certainly not the happiest in nature. – But we are not all born, you know, with the same powers – the same address.' Even more felicitous is his accounting to his mother for Edward's gaucherie: ' "My dear Madam," I always say to her, "you must make yourself easy. The evil is now irremediable, and it has been entirely your own doing." ' She should have sent him to Westminster, with himself, instead of to Mr Pratt's – and Mrs Ferrars, on hearing this, is 'perfectly convinced of her error'.

For such flights as these Mr Collins is too ponderous, and John Thorpe too shallow. The latter's vanity is capable only of the crude boast, for the exercise of which any subject is fitting. His equipage is the most complete of its kind in England, his carriage the neatest, his horse the best goer and himself the best coachman, holding the reins in peculiarly judicious style, and directing the whip with singular discernment and dexterity. His skills in selling horses, racing, shooting and hunting are legendary; and he is able to discompose General Tilney at billiards with what in all modesty he must confess to Catherine was 'one of the cleanest strokes that perhaps ever was made in this world'. Here also, self-praise propagates disparagement. James Morland's gig is a little tittuppy thing without a sound piece of iron about it, the most devilish little ricketty business ever beheld, able to be shaken to pieces at a touch – though in the hands of a good driver like himself capable of being driven to York and back without losing a nail. But the very worst of carriages is, by Jane Austen's invention, revealed as superior to almost any novel in existence. 'Udolpho!' Thorpe cries, upon Catherine's asking him if he has read it. 'Oh, Lord! not I; I never read novels; I have something else to do.' With the exception of *Tom Jones*, Lewis's *Monk* and the writings of

Mrs Radcliffe, he affirms, they are 'the stupidest things in creation'.

Less braggart in tone, naturally, and more dexterously applied, are the speeches employed by more intelligent minds in the self-laudatory task. Isabella Thorpe uses to advantage Catherine's surprise at anything that is exorbitant or questionable in her remarks. Scolding a man for not admiring the angelically beautiful yet amazingly insipid Miss Andrews is thus the enactment of a principle of not loving people by halves, and being ready to do anything for a friend; determination to dress so as to be noticed devolves from the most maidenly rule of never minding what men say. And Catherine's report of Henry Tilney's subdued behaviour in his father's presence during her visit to Milsom-street provides opportunity for her friend's grandiloquent, 'How contemptible! Of all things in the world inconstancy is my aversion.' This concern to cut a figure is what we might expect in Isabella – but not in someone like General Tilney. Yet his purpose, and his method, are the same when he advises Catherine that he cannot pay Henry a visit at Woodston on the Tuesday. It is his club-day; his not attending would be taken amiss; 'and it is a rule with me, Miss Morland, never to give offence to any of my neighbours, if a small sacrifice of time and attention can prevent it.'

Less subtle, but just as efficacious at the right moment, is the direct laying of claim to a particular quality. Mrs Norris's declaring herself a woman of few words and professions, as she begins persuading Sir Thomas to take Fanny into his house, is the more awesome in its prognosticating a plethora of both. Lady Catherine's stated belief, at the diminished table at Rosings, that no one feels the loss of friends as much as she does, is as commanding in its way as her advising Elizabeth in the hermitage at Longbourn House that her character has been celebrated for a sincerity and frankness from which, at such a moment, she will not depart. No less impressive is her telling the assembled company in her drawing room that she supposes few people in England have more enjoyment of music or better taste than she, and that she would have been a great proficient if she had ever learnt.

But a greater proficient even than Lady Catherine at establishing a persona by boastful speech is Mrs Elton. She even outdoes her where music is concerned in being dotingly fond of it and absolutely unable to do without it as a necessity of life. It is one of the resources she is blessed with. Another is her unfailing discernment of what is admirable: she has noted Jane Fairfax's shyness and reserve, and likes her the better for it, being 'a great advocate for timidity' and also sure that one does not often meet with it. The quaint, old-fashioned politeness of Mr Woodhouse delights her; she is often disgusted by modern ease – and has, to boot, 'a vast dislike to puppies', and 'quite a horror of upstarts'. Sound as these views are, moreover, she has not rushed into them. Mrs Elton is as concerned to affect a deliberating independence of opinion as she is to publish the opinions themselves. Since she is one of those who always make their own decisions, she tells Mr Weston, she will judge his son as she finds him; and in announcing to the proud father her pleasure at meeting Frank, adds for his further edification, 'You may believe me. I never compliment.' Jane Fairfax's accomplished performance at the pianoforte thus will provoke, not enchantment, but instead the superbly meditative, 'I do not scruple to say that she plays extremely well.'

However, cogitation quickly fades when other means are called for. Emma learns that adding Jane to the Elton household would not in the least inconvenience its mistress, since her greatest danger perhaps in housekeeping lies in doing too much and being careless of expense; finding Jane a situation will likewise present no difficulty to one of her extensive circle of acquaintance. And the ladies whom Mr Weston bustles off to greet on their arrival at the Crown are certain to be Miss Bates and Jane, because the Elton's coachman and horses are so extremely expeditious: 'I believe we drive faster than anybody.' The confidential boast can do much; but should it falter, a vicarious distinction is to be gained through allusion to Maple Grove, the residence of Mrs Elton's brother Mr Suckling, who flies about amazingly to and from London with four horses and his friend Mr Bragge. If Enscombe, the abode of the Churchills, is the retired place Mr Weston says it is, then it must be like Maple Grove, than which nothing can stand more retired from the road; nor can it be the size of the room at Hartfield which impresses her so much upon her first visit, but its astonishing likeness to the Maple Grove morning room. However, any remaining pretence of discreetness or scruple is at an end when the moment comes for adopting the tones of authority – at a point, for example, where Mrs Weston can be told it will no longer be necessary for her carriage to convey Jane and her aunt, or Emma is silenced with the smiling assurance that only Surrey has ever been called the garden of England; or with the abruptness of an, 'Oh no; the meeting is certainly today'; or with the claim of equality coolly implied in a, 'My dear Miss Woodhouse, a vast deal may be done by those who dare to act. You and I need not be afraid.'

Mrs Elton is supreme through the whole gamut of self-magnification, including the use of the sententious to cover a weakness or inconsistency, or camouflage a purpose. Her never playing despite her passion for music is the result of a married woman having many things to demand her attention; and the natural taste for simplicity which gives her 'quite a horror of finery' springs into existence upon the alarming thought that her dress may be too plain and require a trimming. But she has a close rival in Isabella Thorpe. What could be more affecting than this young lady's plaint – which she makes at finding Catherine Morland determined to keep her appointment with the Tilneys – upon the painfulness of being slighted for strangers when one's own affections are beyond the power of any thing to change? Or her sentiment while Mr Morland's consent to her engagement to James, and his financial assistance, is awaited: 'Had I command of millions, were I mistress of the whole world, your brother would be my only choice'? Mrs Norris, too, must here not be overlooked. Her professions, while more homely, have charming appositeness. To shame Sir Thomas Bertram as he hesitates over bringing Fanny into his household, she discovers that, though far from faultless, she would rather deny herself life's necessities than do an ungenerous thing. Upon the plan being announced later that she should take Fanny at the White house, she becomes a poor, desolate, frail, low-spirited widow; and Lady Bertram's surprise at her resignation to living quite alone cannot move someone who, by further rapid transformation, is fit for nothing but solitude. This pitiable being is just able to live within her income, though she would dearly like to lay a little by the end of the year; but her sister's (for her) energetic, 'I dare say you will. You always do, don't you?' brings the pained and saintly remonstrance, 'My object, Lady Bertram, is to be of use to those that come after me.' *De mortuis nil nisi bonum.*

However much or little Mr Collins may be seen to indulge in these self-glorifying arts and wiles, he will in any case clearly be outdone by other adepts. There is, however, a class of conversation in which he is able to take but small, if any, part, because of the lack of a questioning intelligence – or, as some would doubtless have it, of intelligence itself. This is the variety of lively talk among acquaintances which Mr Bingley's circle would approvingly term an 'argument', and which, if opinion threatened to be too strongly urged, might develop into the kind of 'dispute' for which he had no inclination. Of this nature are the many interesting and amusing discussions which have endeared the novels through their analysis of motives and their commentary on human ways and pleasures – like that in which Elinor Dashwood confesses the many times she has mistaken people's characters by incautiously accepting what is said by others or themselves. These words, seized upon by Marianne as disproving her sister's tenet of subservience to society's judgments, are shown instead to clarify a position upon which the novel itself is founded: 'No, Marianne, never. My doctrine has never aimed at subjection of the understanding. All I have ever attempted to influence has been the behaviour.' In her quiet way Elinor is as redoubtable as Eliza Bennet. Edward Ferrars's airy announcement next morning after his walk to the village that he knows nothing of the picturesque brings upon him her charge of having reacted against the affectations of would-be connoisseurs by a person-al affectation of indifference. He is rescued by Marianne's deploring the artistic jargon which has become so common; but he unrepentantly holds his own, and confounds his deliverer, by stating a simple dislike of 'crooked, twisted, blasted trees', ruined cottages, flourishing weeds and rampant banditti – to Elinor's great amusement.

This is his liveliest moment; and one is reminded by it of the somewhat warmer interchange at Netherfield Park when Bingley modestly seeks to account for his bad handwriting by saying his ideas flow so rapidly that he has not time to express them. Elizabeth's sardonic riposte that his humility must disarm reproof brings into deployment the heavy artillery of Darcy's acumen: nothing is more deceitful, he declares, than that appearance of humility, which is often mere carelessness of opinion, and sometimes the indirect boast – which Bingley's evident pride in his defects of writing shows to be in question. The marshalling of forces proceeds with the inclusion of Bingley's professed likelihood, if he ever quitted Netherfield, of being away within five minutes, and his readiness in principle to jump off his horse the instant a friend requested that he stay another week. Hostilities commence in earnest with a sharp skirmish between Elizabeth and Darcy on whether it is admirable or culpable to yield easily to persuasion. The master of the house is at pains to put a quick stop to the impending battle royal, and does so by comically insisting that the hypothetical friend's size and disposition be taken into account.

Just as much as these sprightly and diverting colloquies, one enjoys the gentler reasonings occasioned by the decencies of friendship and family life. 'That is the happiest conversation,' says Dr Johnson, 'where there is no competition, no vanity, but a calm quiet interchange of sentiments.'[1] Of this kind is the discussion that follows Jane Bennet's engagement to Bingley, when, on Jane's happiness bursting forth in wishes for her sister, Elizabeth replies with a profundity which takes the reader beyond the confines of the novel, 'Till I have your disposition, your goodness, I can never have your happiness' – and then brings him back with her plea to be allowed to shift for herself until another Mr Collins should come along. Or one recalls Mr Knightley and Mrs Weston in conference upon their shared concern for Emma, and anxiously wondering what will happen to her; or the youthful Catherine on the top of Beechen Cliff, so full of love for Henry Tilney and of knowledge, newly acquired in conversing with him, of foregrounds, second distances, sidescreens and perspectives, as voluntarily to reject the whole city of Bath as unworthy to make part of a landscape.

A variety of observation and sentiment arises with the communion of minds. Some critics are little impressed with Fanny Price's enthusiasms; but we would not be without her regret at the absence of anything awful in the chapel at Sotherton, and the discontinuance of the practice of regular prayers in a great house. Memorable, too, is her pleasure when, finding Edmund continuing at the window with her, she speaks her feelings in gazing with him at the stars: 'Here's harmony! Here's repose! Here's what may leave all painting and all music behind, and what poetry can only attempt to describe.' The same emotion, and proximity to a loved one, moves Henry Crawford to discourse on that something in the eloquence of the pulpit which is entitled to the highest respect. And it is the dawning of tenderness for both Louisa and Henrietta Musgrove that inspires Captain Wentworth to record, in rather different style displaying markedly less of reverence, the Admiralty's entertaining themselves now and then with sending a few hundred men to sea in an unseaworthy ship, and his own refined gallantry toward women which is characterised by a refusal to have them aboard.

Romantic attachment is the cause, naturally enough, of a great deal of conversation in the novels, the course of true love leading from instances of positive acrimony to as near the endearments of the betrothed as Jane Austen cares to take us. Some of the most entertaining, as well as informative, speeches come in the series of embroilments which breaks out as Mary Crawford, walking with Edmund and Fanny, pictures the Mrs Eleanors and Mrs Bridgets of former days starched up in seeming piety in Sotherton's chapel, their thoughts certainly not occupied with the chaplain who would have been inferior even to the parsons of the present. Her comment provokes discussion as to whether private prayer, being easier, is preferable to prayer in public. Henry's dictum that a mind which will not struggle against itself under one set of circumstances is unlikely to prevail in others goes for the moment unchallenged; but he is soon to be assailed by the scorn for parsonical motive implied in Mary's sudden, 'There is a very good living kept for you, I understand, hereabouts.' He admits inevitable bias through the knowledge that provision has been made for him, but argues that this is no pointer to insincerity in a profession offering small worldly advantage. For his pains he is accused of preferring an income ready-made to the trouble of working for one, and of joining a body of men universally looked down upon. Debate of Mary's thesis that 'where an opinion is general, it is usually correct' is cut short by Fanny's exclaiming at the kindness William has met with from the chaplain of the *Antwerp*, but the conflict is to be renewed later; for it not only arises out of strong mutual feelings of attraction, but is charged with romantic meaning for the contenders.

It is only to be expected, amongst cultured and intelligent beings living beneath the precise regulations which their society decreed for the conduct of the sexes, that a diplomacy as to romance will be one of the arts of conversation. Someone as apparently staid as Edmund proves he can use it in this purpose as ably as the flirtatious Henry Crawford himself. As talk at the Parsonage comes round to matters of economy, Mary Crawford makes her assertion that a large income is the best recipé for happiness she has ever heard of, and goes on to declare her contempt for honest poverty and preference for honest wealth and distinction. Edmund answers her, in serious tone, that there are distinctions he desires and would be miserable at not attaining, but that they are of a different character. Fanny sees with a pang some reflection on Miss Crawford's side of his 'look of consciousness as he spoke'; but Mary's response does not come until the dinner party Dr Grant gives the Bertrams, when discussion during the game of Speculation centres upon possible improvements to Thornton

Lacey. Edmund rejects Henry's plans, saying he intends to make the house comfortable and attractive without any heavy expense: 'that must suffice me; and I hope may suffice all who care about me.' The sentiment, and the tone of voice and half-look with which it is uttered, move Mary hastily to secure William Price's knave at an exorbitant rate, and to exclaim, 'There, I will stake my last like a woman of spirit. No cold prudence for me.' The game resumes, the resolve conveyed in her words lost on all but Edmund and Fanny.

Henry Crawford's very considerable powers are enlivened with humour. In the drawing room at Mansfield Park, where he has been reading Shakespeare aloud, he catches at the suggestion Lady Bertram makes in complimenting him that he should fit up a theatre at his house in Norfolk:

> 'Do you, Ma'am?' cried he with quickness. 'No, no, that will never be. Your Ladyship is quite mistaken. No theatre at Everingham! Oh! no.' – And he looked at Fanny with an expressive smile, which evidently meant, 'that lady will never allow a theatre at Everingham.'

Edmund sees both what is meant and Fanny's determination not to see it, and decides that 'such a ready comprehension of a hint' is favourable to Henry's hopes. With far less aplomb does Mr Elton try the same thing, as Emma tells how Isabella's reluctant approval of her portrait of John Knightley caused her to make the resolution against portraiture which she will now break on Harriet's account, there being 'no husbands and wives in the case at present'. Elton seizes upon the phrase with an 'Exactly so – no husbands and wives', and with a consciousness so interesting that Emma begins to consider whether she had not better leave him and Harriet together at once.

There is here none of the finesse observable on that hot summer day at Sotherton Court when Henry Crawford pays his addresses to the bespoken Maria Bertram with circuitous eloquence. He has made an admirable preface in the chapel by stating, in the lady's hearing, a dislike of seeing Miss Bertram so near the altar – and, upon her inquiring as soon as she has regained composure if he will give her away, a conviction that he should do so very awkwardly. Before the locked iron gate in the pleasure grounds, having contrived to get Mr Rushworth sent off to find the key, he tells her that he thinks he will never see Sotherton with as much pleasure as he does now; and on being assured, after a moment's embarrassment on the lady's part, that a man of the world will see it improved, as others do, he claims feelings too little evanescent, and a memory rather too ungovernable for him to merit the category. Soon, his reference to the smiling prospect before her eyes draws from Maria a confession of the 'feeling of restraint and hardship' the gate and the ha-ha cause; and Crawford's judicious reminder of Mr Rushworth's 'authority and protection', coupled with the assertion that she can get out easily with his own assistance if this is not prohibited, leads her to commitment with the words, 'Prohibited! nonsense! I certainly can get out that way, and I will.' Though the nature of the subject, perfectly understood by Fanny, arouses a flushed protest from her and disapproval in ourselves, the parley's sophistication, and indeed delicacy, cannot fail to impress.

A Louisa Musgrove is not to be compared with a Maria Bertram; but she must be to some extent aware, as she strolls with Captain Wentworth at Winthrop, that in discussing herself and her sentiments with a man to whom she is becoming increasingly attached, she is making an appeal to his heart: for this, in Jane Austen's terms, is an 'interesting' conversation that by its nature can but hint at romance. Yet Louisa is not really acting by design when she takes up Captain Wentworth's jest at his sister's indifference to being overturned by Admiral Croft's gigmanship, and professes eagerly a like bruising devotion to the man she should love. She speaks here with naturalness and on impulse; one must wonder, though, whether there might not be something more purposive in her condemning Henrietta's readiness to yield to Mary's haughty persuasions and give up her visit to Winthrop, and to Charles Hayter. Certainly what she has to say brings Wentworth's approval of the decision and firmness of character it denotes – such warmth of congratulation and advice, indeed, as can leave the attendant Anne Elliot in no doubt as to what Louisa must be feeling. The reappearance of Henrietta with the happy Charles Hayter is not the only thing that marks out Louisa for Captain Wentworth from then onwards.

It is from the heart – though it be a troubled heart – that Wentworth has spoken: true feeling must find expression. But, at certain times and in certain places, love cannot directly declare itself, and is compelled to suggest and insinuate. Even when Wentworth, sure now of his wishes, is standing beside Anne Elliot in the freedom which the Octagon Room's space and bustle of public thoroughfare affords, he can only glance at his own thoughts by speaking of his surprise that Captain Benwick should turn to someone like Louisa after having loved 'a very superior creature' like Fanny Harville. 'A man does not recover from such a devotion of the heart to such a woman!' he exclaims. ' – He ought not – he does not.' Anne cannot speak; and he, uncertain as to her attitude and affections, can say no more -- but he has said much. No less meaningful, or fraught with emotion, are the few words Anne exchanges later on with Mrs Musgrove at the White Hart on the subject of putting off the play till Tuesday so that they can all attend the party Sir Walter and Elizabeth are giving in Camden-place. She states her small inclination for the party and readiness to go to the theatre in Mrs Musgrove's company, while acknowledging the difficulty they would find in the proceeding. The remark is inconsequential in itself – 'but she trembled when it was done, conscious that her words were listened to, and daring not even to try to observe their effect.' The effect is immediate: Captain Wentworth is at her side, speaking with new decision, and only Henrietta's hurrying in to interrupt the group can prevent his avowal.

In the end it is Anne who declares her love, through a masterly hinting during the course of conversation in the same apartment, where she has arrived to find Mrs Musgrove talking to Mrs Croft, and Captain Harville to Captain Wentworth, and Mary and Henrietta expected to join the party at any moment. She can only sit, outwardly composed but plunged in agitation, listening to the talk of others until she is herself beckoned into conversation by Captain Harville as he takes from its parcel the miniature of Captain Benwick, first drawn for his sister, and now destined for Louisa Musgrove. The trembling words, 'Poor Fanny! she would not have forgotten him so soon!' are the beginning of a discussion – of an 'argument' – upon love and devotion in men and women which takes increasing significance from the well-defined social situation – and the motionless figure of Captain Wentworth as he sits poised, pen in hand, striving to catch sounds which Anne thinks for a moment might not be reaching him. She has started smilingly with an assured, 'We certainly do not forget you, so soon as you forget us,' justifying it by a kindly contrasting of the confined lives of women with the exertions which men face in their careers; soon she and Harville are engaged in the deepest analysis of human feelings, each claiming for their sex strength and endurance in affection upon the analogy of the bodily frames of men and women, and by the verdict of literature, until the impossibility of proof confronts them. It is when Harville tries to describe the love of a sailor for his wife and family ashore – speaking 'only of such men as have hearts!' as he presses his own with emotion – that Anne is driven by the logic of debate and of her love for Wentworth to concede the point and to make, while composure lasts, an assertion of love undying:

> 'Oh!' cried Anne eagerly, 'I hope I do justice to all that is felt by you, and those who resemble you. God forbid that I should undervalue the warm and faithful feelings of any of my fellow-creatures. I should deserve utter contempt if I dared to suppose that true attachment and constancy were known only by woman. No, I believe you capable of every thing great and good in your married lives. I believe you equal to every important exertion, and to every domestic forbearance, so long as – if I may be allowed the expression, so long as you have an object. I mean, while the woman you love lives, and lives for you. All the privilege I claim for my own sex (it is not a very enviable one, you need not covet it) is that of loving longest, when existence or when hope is gone.'

The speeches of Juliet herself are not more frank, tender or affecting than this of Anne Elliot, considered in its setting: for, with proper respect to decorum, she must woo her man through the screen of social circumstance by the skills of eloquence and simplicity of truth, without directing an overt word to him.

The ability to hint with delicacy at romantic attachment is not to be expected in Mr Collins. He has, one would think, neither the mental nor the emotional accomplishment for nurturing the art – though he does possess a command of words which might otherwise have stood him in good stead. What he manages to intimate to Charlotte Lucas at the dinner party the Bennets give her family to make her almost certain by the time it breaks up that her plan will succeed, we shall unfortunately never know. But there can, surely, be little room for hinting in association with so massive a self-regard. Mr Collins's wish, upon his arrival at Longbourn, to avoid appearing forward and precipitate on the subject of making amends to his fair cousins takes the alarming form of an assurance to the young ladies that he comes prepared to admire them. 'At present I will not say more,' he continues with thunderous caution, 'but perhaps when we are better acquainted – ' A fortunate summons to dinner saves the family from the full revelation of his discretionary powers.

What Mr Collins in fact excels at is the address indiscreet and confessional. This distinction of being able to make common property of his inmost thoughts he shares with Miss Bates; but whereas actual ideas have to be searched for in her speeches amidst the welter of irrelevant material, Mr Collins's thinking is presented to his hearers in a manner engagingly pointed and precise. Thus when Mr Bennet receives an olive branch through the post, or when his daughter is favoured by a proposal of marriage, neither is left to guess at the motive. A wealth of personal information is laid at Elizabeth's feet: she is not only told of her suitor's having come with the intention of selecting a wife, and of his reasons for wishing to marry – among them being the expectation that it will add greatly to his happiness – but is made familiar with the exact terms and tones of Lady Catherine's prompting: 'Chuse properly, chuse a gentlewoman for *my* sake; and for your *own*, let her be an active, useful sort of person, not brought up high, but able to make a small income go a good way.' That what is at work here is not some rare genus of an otherwise exemplary candour, but an insensibility almost as rare, is clear from Mr Collins's ascribing Elizabeth's refusal, at the end of the interview, to her wish of increasing his love by suspense, 'according to the usual practice of elegant females'. She and her father have been under no illusion from the moment of their visitor's grave disclosure of his method of composing and delivering compliments to ladies.

Other people's feelings do not enter into Mr Collins's calculations – and scarcely into his consciousness. His near-perfect self-involvement is apparent not only when he holds the centre of the stage, but even in his exits and his entrances. It is announced in his letter telling Mr Bennet that the week's visit he proposes therein can be made 'without any inconvenience' since his patroness has no objection to his occasional absence from Hunsford. He enlivens his departure by accepting as renewed invitation Mrs Bennet's polite expression of happiness in seeing him at some future time, and sending in his letter of thanks the comforting explanation that he has done so merely with the view of enjoying the company of Charlotte Lucas. Aware of what she is dealing with, Elizabeth has come near to discouraging Mr Collins's amatory pursuit by suggesting that Lady Catherine will be displeased at her lack of qualification for the honour. Mrs Bennet, by ignorance, attains greater success in her outburst at her daughter's perversity. 'Pardon me for interrupting you, Madam,' the suitor cries, 'but if she is really headstrong and foolish, I know not whether she would altogether be a very desirable wife to a man in my situation, who naturally looks for happiness in the marriage state.' It is thus to be foreseen that in welcoming Elizabeth to Hunsford Mr Collins should speak to her as if wishing to make her feel what she has lost in refusing him; or that he should presume, in writing to Mr Bennet after Lydia's elopement, 'to reflect with augmented satisfaction on a certain event of last November, for had it been otherwise, I must have been involved in all your sorrow and disgrace.' Lack of discretion in this degree must be set down as pure folly. There is something curiously engaging, though, in the trust it implies in the value of every notion, and in the almost regal freedom through which these firstlings of the brain are scattered for others' edification.

If his achievements in self-revelation are set on one side, Mr Collins's speeches are seen to be limited in their range and uninspired in their quality when viewed beside typical modes of utterance in the novels. They show him to be, in sophistication, intelligence and moral quality, far removed from the best of the characters, though by no means so bad as the worst. Whatever social blunders he may commit, a complaisant manner ensures that many of the excesses of arrogance to be found in the pronouncements of others are avoided. His assumption of excellence, oddly enough, also helps to chasten his remarks. The crude boast is absent. If he is inclined to talk without ceasing of his house and garden at Hunsford, or to invite Elizabeth to admire everything within them, it is with a sense of wonder at his fortunate lot and an evident wish that such contentment might be spread abroad. There is no seeking for status in one whose dearest aspirations seem to be satisfied. He may name Rosings as frequently as Mrs Elton calls to aid Maple Grove, but his comparisons, unlike hers, are not odious: when he declares upon entering Mrs Philips's house that he might almost have supposed himself in Lady Catherine's small summer breakfast parlour, his aim is chiefly to flatter his hostess. And when that good lady learns that the chimneypiece alone in one of the drawing rooms at Rosings had cost eight hundred pounds, she feels the full force of the compliment, 'and would hardly have resented a comparison with the housekeeper's room.'

Similarly, there is in Mr Collins no such pressing desire to lay claim to perfections as can motivate persons as different as General Tilney and Isabella Thorpe. He does, it is true, assert his skill in the art of compliment – but the subject is mentioned in passing and pursued only through Mr Bennet's persistent questioning. Much the same applies to his boasting himself better qualified by education and habitual study to decide upon social niceties than his cousin Elizabeth: the claim only comes after she has implied the contrary in trying to stop him introducing himself to Mr Darcy. That he can be deficient in any way does not admit of question; his speeches are almost quite free of protestations designed to hide a weakness. The exceptions are those assurances of bearing Lydia no ill-will for interrupting his reading of Fordyce's Sermons, or of not resenting the behaviour of Elizabeth in turning down his proposal, or of not in the least regarding his losses at whist – all which, made in a manner or with a tone of voice indicating the contrary, are Mr Collins's way of reining in those impulses that might cause him to swerve from the path of rectitude.

But there is a tendency to be found in Mr Collins's statements which has no place in those of most of the other characters: a touch, not of steel, certainly, but of a stringency which entices him towards the captious. The truth, which he records with a certain sternness, that young ladies are little interested in books of a serious stamp despite there being nothing so advantageous to them as instruction, is made the means of mild rebuke. So is the more painful fact of Elizabeth's indifference to him, in leading him to reflect with some contentment upon unattained benefits found to be illusory. These less than civil reflections Mr Collins presents with his usual guileless candour, but they are followed by others more forcefully frank; and deepening acquaintance reveals in him a censoriousness which is the more trenchant (and diverting) in being divorced from discretion.

Thus, in condoling by letter with his cousin upon the grievous affliction of Lydia's elopement, he comments on the reason there is to think that the girl's licentious conduct 'has proceeded from a faulty degree of indulgence' – adding, however, for the consolation of Mr Bennet and his wife, that Lydia's own disposition must be naturally bad, as she could not otherwise be guilty of such an enormity at so early an age. He ends by coupling pity for the distressed parents with the certainty that this false step in one daughter 'will be injurious to the fortunes of all the others, for who, as lady Catherine herself condescendingly says, will connect themselves to such a family'. This is as round as need be, but the masterstroke of reprobation in the next letter is reserved for Lydia's father: it is nothing less than a set-down, to which Mr Bennet's own is a retort.

> 'I must not, however, neglect the duties of my station, or refrain from declaring my amazement, at hearing that you received the young couple into your house as soon as they were married. It was an encouragement of vice; and had I been the rector of Longbourn, I should very strenuously have opposed it.'

This indignation is of the righteous kind. The discarding of meekness in favour of the posture militant is brought about in Mr Collins by what he feels to be pastoral obligation. It was this which, if he is to be believed, first sent him on his way to the Bennets to spread the blessing of peace, and, indeed, which forms the basis of his estimate of himself. As he assures the perplexed Elizabeth, he considers the clerical office 'as equal in point of dignity with the highest rank in the kingdom – provided that a proper humility of behaviour is at the same time maintained'. The only vaunt that he is prepared to make – one bemusing in its effect – is about his status as a clergyman.

The two most prominent aspects of his personality are united in the address which, to Elizabeth's embarrassment and her father's delight, Mr Collins declaims in a loud voice to the entire company in the ballroom at Netherfield after Mr Darcy has rebuffed his attempt to introduce himself. It is a masterpiece of presumptuous lowliness. Choosing the moment after Mary's debacle at the pianoforte when others are being asked for a musical contribution, he begins in his patroness's mode by declaring that an air would certainly be forthcoming from him if he were so fortunate as to be able to sing. This light introduction makes way for the august theme of a clergyman's manifold responsibilities, the dominant motif of obtaining an advantageous agreement on tithes ushering in the lesser refrains of sermon-writing, parish preoccupations, and improvements to the parsonage. But the profounder statement is yet to come. The necessity of conciliatory manners towards every body, especially those to whom the cleric owes preferment, is set forth with a commanding resonance which makes all the more affecting the diminuendo of the concluding passage: 'I cannot acquit him of that duty; nor could I think well of the man who should omit an occasion of testifying his respect towards any body connected with the family.' The performer's bow brings by way of applause stares, smiles, and Mrs Bennet's commendations on the sensibleness of the remarks and the cleverness of the speaker.

Her judgment in the latter comment might be defended. Mr Collins has replied to Darcy's rudeness by an admirably impersonal allusion to his clerical responsibilities. It is thus unexceptionable in being perfectly polite; but as a retort and a self-vindication it is also emphatic. For not only does it justify his earlier conduct, but it infers a claim to social recognition and to station which, though of a kind subordinate to Darcy's own, ought nevertheless to command his respect.

Is the claim spurious? Darcy reacts to Mr Collins's social intrusion as one imagines Sir Walter Elliot would have responded to any familiarity from Mr Wentworth, the curate of Monkford. The term gentleman is hardly to be applied to such persons: Edmund Bertram's intention to make one of their number induces in Mary Crawford the near-horror implicit in her assertion, 'A clergyman is nothing.' Whatever he may urge on behalf of those who have charge of all that is of first importance to both the individual and society, temporally and eternally, Edmund cannot alter Mary's conviction that what makes men clergymen is a love of ease, an absence of ambition, and a deplorable manner. In her confidence that she is speaking the general opinion she is on firm ground. Only the rare mortal in the society presented in Jane Austen's novels appreciates the dignity of the clerical calling and function. Edmund's father is thus distinguished. When Henry Crawford makes known his wish to become the tenant of Thornton Lacey, on the assumption that Edmund will as a matter of course be an absentee parson, he receives a crushing rejoinder. Sir Thomas will be 'deeply mortified' if his son does not live in his own parish. Human nature, he tells Crawford, needs, more than weekly sermons, the friendship of the pastor: if he does not live amongst his people, 'he does very little either for their good or his own.' And he concludes with a deliberating courtesy that is eloquent of the clergyman's true status: 'Thornton Lacey is the only house in the neighbourhood in which I should *not* be happy to wait on Mr Crawford as occupier.'

Much as Mr Collins might be despised in the minds of his hearers at Netherfield, he is not at fault in affirming the parson's right to consideration. From many points of view the stand he takes is as defensible as that of Elizabeth Bennet in vindicating the right of younger daughters not to be socially handicapped by the custom of coming out. Perhaps like her own, though, his choice of time and place is not beyond criticism.

There is thus something original, and even vivacious, in the readiness which he reveals by word and action to break with the conventions – though always, be it understood, where his own interests are involved. It is not solely in escaping out of Longbourn House with admirable slyness in order to hasten to Lucas Lodge and there throw himself at Charlotte's feet that the 'fire and independence of his character' is apparent. But his speeches as a whole demonstrate a quality which must be creditable, and may be deemed admirable, in any human being, even if it will not normally lead to advancement and fortune. In Mr Collins's statements, be they civil or ceremonious, trivial or platitudinous, laughably presumptuous or stupidly contentious, there is almost a complete absence of pretence. Amidst his many shortcomings he is sincere, and, happily, nearly always transparently so. There is an element of the paradisal in its scarcely ever occurring to him that a covering is requisite for the nakedness of his thoughts. In this not insignificant respect Mr Collins appears as an innocent – though, doubtless, he is one of those who will not 'scape the thunderbolt of the reader's derision.

7

Romance

The follies and shortcomings so far considered do not include
the main charge against Mr Collins. He may be acquitted on
some counts, perhaps on others granted pardon; but of the chief
we must think that nothing can ever clear him, because it is a
matter of his sins against love. Here we come to the head and
front of his offence. His clumsiness and bungling in the affairs of
the heart may be diverting, but the laughter cannot obscure his
hatefulness as the smug enemy of romance. For in that gentle
and gracious realm he shows himself a churlish intruder.

True, others who enter there are not always presented in a
prepossessing light. John Dashwood's uxoriousness is no more
appealing than other of his characteristics; James Morland we
learn little of, perhaps because there is little to tell; Edmund
Bertram we must admire, but cannot imagine as a lover;
Edward Ferrars's passivity makes it hard to understand what
Elinor Dashwood sees in him; Mr Elton lets us down as much as
he does Emma in his two-facedness and self-seeking; Colonel
Brandon we rule out as promptly as Marianne does at first,
flannel waistcoat or no; and Mr Knightley, despite all his manly
virtues, is not a Romeo, or even a Mr Darcy. Those flawed
gems Willoughby and Wickham are by that very fact more
life-like and more interesting: they readily carry the spirit of
romance while acting out of ruthlessly selfish motive. Yet they
all either can and do undergo the emotion of love, or are able at
least to inspire it. Mr Collins can achieve neither. His reflections
and way of conducting himself seem to distance him from even
the possibility of tenderness; the mere thought of him being run
away with by his feelings reduces Elizabeth Bennet to helpless
mirth. Among the persons of novels treating of courtship and
marriage he is therefore an oddity – but with hints of the

nefarious. There is the damning evidence of his behaviour in proposing to Elizabeth with a suddenness and assurance which disgusts, with gross insensitivity to her finer feelings and her dislike, and with a heartless disregard which will not only scorn her refusal but expatiate on her poor matrimonial prospects. Laughable Mr Collins may be: but he is revealed as an offender against the very soul of romantic attachment.

How very different he is from Mr Darcy is apparent, if proof were needed, from the abject failure of the one in his suit, and the merited and moving success of the other. But a disquieting state of affairs comes into view if we compare, not the men, but the proposals they make to Elizabeth. For they are strikingly similar. Mr Darcy is just as sudden as Mr Collins; his avowal is just as unexpected by the lady; he is as completely unaware of her keen disapproval of his manners and actions – that her feelings in every respect forbid acceptance; if possible, he is the object of a more cordial dislike; and, for good measure, he contrives to speak with an eloquence upon the subject of Elizabeth's socially disadvantaged condition that surpasses Mr Collins's own. Mr Darcy may not be a Mr Collins at heart, but he almost out-Collins Collins in paying his addresses.

Even more extraordinary is Darcy's sharing this doubtful distinction with others – or rather, Mr Collins's mode being so seemingly prevalent. The 'blush of surprise' which his request-ing the interview causes in Elizabeth may be compared to the astonishment 'beyond expression' with which she later greets Darcy's proposal, the 'interesting silence' from being 'too completely overpowered to be immediately able to reply' with which Emma hears the expression of Mr Elton's hopes, and Fanny Price's state of 'astonishment and confusion', of being 'for some moments unable to speak' through her extreme distress at Henry Crawford's making a declaration she regards as mere trifling and 'nonsense' intended to deceive.

In all these instances of devotion declared there is the utmost surprise on the part of the heroine, by whom they are entirely unexpected, and to whom they are as equally unwelcome because of intense dislike for the man who is speaking. That such sensitive and intelligent young women should have no idea of the feelings the gentlemen entertain towards them is almost as hard to credit as the fact that in each case the gentleman is perfectly confident of being accepted – without, apparently, being on such terms with the lady as might give him grounds for assurance. If we include the self-doubting Mr Knightley, whom Emma scarcely dislikes, but whose unforeseen declaration is just as effective in making her 'absolutely silent' with amazedness, there are in Jane Austen's six major novels up to six examples of proposals being made to astonished heroines on the basis of no understanding whatsoever.

Mr Collins's courting of Elizabeth Bennet greatly amuses us: but his manner, and the reaction it provokes, are not exceptional within the novels' world. This is most strange; we can scarcely think it possible; but the mere fact – as fact it is – points to a system of social forms and conduct which we do not readily grasp – and to the further fact that Mr Collins, while himself scarcely typical of that world, is curiously not unrepresentative of it.

Never, in her wildest exercises of imagination or in her dreams, has Emma thought that Mr Knightley looked upon her with a lover's affection; yet he has done so throughout. But she has wrongly anticipated being proposed to by a younger man whose behaviour is marked by a gallantry and friendly ease – no more – and whose few uncertain words at a moment of leavetaking create certainty in her. Of course, though her heart is untouched she has fallen victim to Frank Churchill's design of diverting attention from his secret engagement to Jane Fairfax; but is it not significant, even so, that a young woman of her capacity and discernment has been so completely in the dark about her situation *vis-à-vis* three men? for the disagreeable Mr Elton must be taken into the reckoning. Ought we to conclude that Emma's over-active mind has been deceiving her with regard to all three – and, presumably, that Elizabeth Bennet has been too blinded by resentment to realise that Darcy is in love with her?

But what, then, is to be said of Catherine Morland, who is neither brainy nor emotional? After almost a month's stay at

Northanger she believes Henry Tilney's family love her, and is somewhat less sure about his feelings; but, young as she is, she has already been accused – to her great perplexity – of pointedly favouring a young man, if not of accepting his advances. Before leaving Bath she has been applied to by Isabella Thorpe on behalf of her brother John, to whom, she says, Catherine has given 'the most positive encouragement'. The letter his sister received claims that John has as good as made an offer, while Catherine has responded to his addresses 'in the kindest way'. Of such conduct, in John Thorpe and in herself, Catherine is totally unaware, and

> with all the earnestness of truth, expressed her astonishment at such a charge, protesting her innocence of every thought of Mr Thorpe's being in love with her, and the consequent impossibility of her having ever intended to encourage him.

She has been insensible of receiving any attention from him, and can only account for the idea of a declaration being made by supposing some unaccountable mistake. Now John Thorpe is a rattle and braggart, unreliable in his opinions and capable of bending fact to his wishes; but we must set him down as nothing but a buffoon – indeed, as entirely in the grip of illusion – if his action in a matter of this sort is without some basis.

Might it not rather be in accord with the evidence which the novels provide to see Jane Austen's romantic realm as one where ignorance as to the feelings of others and error as to their motives are not only easily possible, but likely; where the rigidities governing manners, and especially the social relations of the sexes, normally make so difficult the establishing of sympathetic understanding as to create a medium which is little short of treacherous?

Signs are there, if we will heed them, of an area of human dealings hedged about with impediments, where to venture is to incur the risk either of deep embarrassment or of unbridled derision. Marianne Dashwood, for instance, sees less of the person of her rescuer Willoughby than the rest of her family, for the reason that the confusion which crimsoned over her face upon his carrying her down the hill 'had robbed her of the power of regarding him after their entering the house'. Such are modesty's compulsions in an informal contact between man and woman. Her blushing consciousness is in keeping with the behaviour of people in general where romance is suspected. We tend to see little wider significance in Isabella Thorpe's ability to 'discover a flirtation between any gentleman and lady who only smiled on each other' amidst the fashionable crowds of Bath, and Mrs Jennings's relish in quickly perceiving supposed attachments, and 'raising the blushes and vanity of many a young lady' by her insinuations: we dismiss these tasteless and oddly immature feats as tokens of their vulgarity. So they may be; but the attitude that produces them is the rule. Colonel Brandon's alleged partiality for Marianne receives the 'attention and wit' of all his friends at Barton Park; their raillery is only drawn away from him by Willoughby's apparent triumph with the lady – at the point when Brandon's feelings really begin to call for what Jane Austen, with scorn, terms, 'the ridicule so justly annexed to sensibility'. This state of things decrees that a correspondence by letter between an unmarried man and woman indicates their being engaged, and 'could be authorised by nothing else': so, at least, Elinor understands Edward's writing to Lucy Steele. And it ensures that a lady who displays a liking which is not followed by a proposal from the man so favoured should receive from the world, not its compassion as we might expect, but, according to Elizabeth Bennet, its 'derision for disappointed hopes'.

The very language of the seducer can add its testimony concerning the climate of the times. Catherine Morland, to her indignation, catches the murmured words of Captain Tilney to her friend Isabella when he sits down by her in the Pump Room. His complaint of being watched provoking Isabella to declare her independence of spirit, he replies by wishing her heart were independent. That sentiment is dismissed by the lady on the grounds that, 'You men have none of you any hearts.' Tilney responds with, 'If we have not hearts, we have eyes; and they give us torment enough'; and upon Isabella's turning mocking-ly away with the jibe that his eyes are thereby no longer tormented, she is assured, 'Never more so; for the edge of a blooming cheek is still in view – at once too much and too little.' The manner of this boldness, tentative and oblique despite the obligingness of its object, is indicative of the force of those prohibitions and pressures it seeks to defy.

A relaxation of attitude by man or woman is fraught with peril, though it come well short of familiarity. Mrs Bennet's hopes for Jane are kindled by the mere fact that Bingley has 'actually danced with her twice' at a public ball – though her thinking upon this theme is admittedly of incandescent quality. Isabella Thorpe, however, is no less aware of the niceties. Having declined to dance with Charles Hodges on the strength of her so far unauthorised engagement to the absent James Morland, she promptly accepts the arm of Captain Tilney – because, she explains to the puzzled Catherine, to have continued sitting still 'would have looked so particular; and you know how I abhor doing that.' It is with comparable sense of propriety, if Mrs Norris is to be believed, that Maria Bertram had danced only two dances out of four with Mr Rushwort at the impromptu ball at Mansfield. His mother as she looks on feels it a pity that the common forms should have been allowed to part the couple in the present situation; but Mrs Norris turns the matter to advantage by replying that 'dear Maria has such a strict sense of propriety, so much of that true delicacy which one seldom meets with now-a-days, Mrs Rushworth, that wish of avoiding particularity!' No desire can be more laudable in a young woman. Its absence in Marianne Dashwood, who, speedily recovered from her embarrassment, is talking to Willoughby with great unreserve before the end of his next visit, prompts Elinor's reproaches. But her sister contemns the prudence which would have had her 'reserved, spiritless, dull, and deceitful' instead of being open and sincere, and proceeds to give Willoughby patent assurance of regard in response to his frank admiration. This public demonstration of attachment Elinor properly deplores. She will not even tolerate a show of affection when the three sisters, as they walk along the road through Barton valley, descry an approaching horseman whom Marianne, thinking it to be Willoughby, rushes forward to meet. Elinor doubts the identification, and with sisterly devotion quickens her pace and keeps up with the hurrying girl, in order 'to screen Marianne from particularity'.

Jane Austen does not hide her amusement at Richardson's maxim that no lady can be justified in falling in love before the gentleman's love is declared; but nowhere does she doubt the appropriateness of behaving as if the maxim were true. It is the unquestioned assumption of her heroines and of the society in which they move that correct conduct for a young woman in men's company implies the preservation of a decorous frigidity. In the best-known instance, Elizabeth Bennet considers with pleasure that Jane's affection for Bingley is unlikely to be perceived by the world in general, since her sister's composure and equanimity will 'guard her from the suspicions of the impertinent'. Charlotte Lucas does not share her friend's satisfaction: a woman, she argues, who for fear of society's scorn conceals her feelings, and will not encourage her man in his first intimations of fondness by showing even more affection than she feels, will be in danger of losing him. The worst of course happens. Darcy, anxious for the interests of his friend, observes Jane narrowly at the Netherfield ball and finds in her no 'symptom of peculiar regard': she has received Bingley's attentions with pleasure, but not so as to invite them 'by any noticeable participation of sentiment'. Whether Darcy is truly objective, or sees what he wishes to see, is a question in his own mind when he writes to Elizabeth.

The same kind of scrutiny is applied to his niece by Sir Thomas Bertram when they are dining with the Grants. Crawford's confession of an attachment to the Bertram family that is increasingly important to him causes Sir Thomas to watch the reaction of the person at whom all understand the compliment to be aimed. Fanny's reception of it 'was so proper and modest, so calm and uninviting, that he had nothing to censure in her.' He assumes, of course, that it is welcome to Fanny, when in fact she detests it; but her manner of dispassionateness, of cool indifference, is approved as being entirely fitting in the acceptance of this attention. Edmund is less sanguine when he, too, watches Crawford and Fanny later to see 'what degree of immediate encouragement for him might be extracted from her manners': the minimal responsiveness which had so impressed his father makes him almost ready to wonder at his friend's perseverance.

But in no way is her admirer discouraged. On the contrary, Fanny's display of due feminine reserve increases both his ardour and his confidence. Her behaviour during the interview authorised by Sir Thomas in which Crawford proposes is interpreted as favourable, if not held to be encouraging: 'her conduct at this very time, by speaking the disinterestedness and delicacy of her character (qualities which he believed most rare indeed), was of a sort to heighten all his wishes, and confirm all his resolutions.' This adjudgment is helped, according to the author, by the vanity which inclines Crawford to think she must love him, and by the operation of an active, sanguine spirit in making a withheld affection appear of greater consequence. But if this is so in Crawford, why should it not be true of Mr Collins? If he is less active and buoyant of spirit, he has perhaps even more self-conceit; and has he not with equal appreciation discovered in Elizabeth a 'natural delicacy' which, though it must needs lead her to 'dissemble', betokens a degree of excellence in the female character?

Henry Crawford is conscious of addressing a woman still not mature, guarded by a youth of mind as lovely as of person, 'whose modesty had prevented her from understanding his attentions'. But Mr Collins here exceeds him. Not only does he entertain similar notions concerning Elizabeth, but he puts them inimitably into words: 'Believe me, my dear Miss Elizabeth, that your modesty, so far from doing you any disservice, rather adds to your other perfections. You would have been less amiable in my eyes had there *not* been this little unwillingness.' An obstacle in love's path must increase ardour, even if the lover is Mr Collins. His state may be less interesting than that of Crawford, who, in commencing his addresses after giving Fanny news of her brother's promotion, has been forced to part from her upon Sir Thomas's unexpected appearance 'at a moment when her modesty alone seemed to his sanguine and pre-assured mind to stand in the way of the happiness he sought'. However, if Mr Collins's feelings are not so tyrannous, they are none the less attributable to a shared human nature, and to a concept of feminine behaviour and charm which he and Crawford just as truly share.

Guardedness where the other sex is concerned is requisite in man, as in woman. Henry Crawford shows mastery in his early dealings with the Bertram sisters: to each he is lively and agreeable in a way which loses him no ground with either, but which just stops short of 'the consistence, the steadiness, the solicitude, and the warmth which might excite general notice', or be misconstrued as a sign of attachment. Mr Elton, while not displaying as much adroitness, is just as wary. The moment his engagement to Miss Augusta Hawkins is announced, he is able to confront all the young ladies of Highbury with cordial, fearless smiles, when a few weeks before he would have been 'more cautiously gallant'. But Captain Wentworth is nothing other than an object-lesson. The quarter-deck, by training him in free and natural ways, has made him a bit of a menace in the drawing room; not that there is anything improper in his attitude, but that he does not calculate the effects of an engagingness of manner upon the feminine heart. He would have come to Kellynch and Uppercross better prepared for peacetime encounters, one must think, if he had arrived at Lisbon a week later the previous spring, and been obliged to convey Lady Grierson and her daughters. Anne Elliot quickly sees how desirable it is that he should know his own mind early enough to avoid endangering the happiness of either of the Musgrove girls; and without hesitation, when Charles Hayter's discomfiture is apparent, she finds Wentworth 'wrong in accepting the attentions – (for accepting must be the word) of two young women at once'. He is shocked when his error presents itself to him in Captain Harville's considering him an engaged man. Unwittingly, he had entangled himself. 'I had not considered that my excessive intimacy must have its danger of ill consequence in many ways,' he confesses to Anne at the end: 'and that I had no right to be trying whether I could attach myself to either of the girls, at the risk of raising even an unpleasant report, were there no other ill effects.'

Captain Wentworth is guilty of an extreme in indiscretion.

For under the stringencies which govern conduct in Jane Austen's society, trifles light as air in a man's behaviour towards them can appear to women's quick apprehensions as proofs of love – as they not infrequently are. The paying of social calls can signify much. That Darcy and Colonel Fitzwilliam should accompany Mr Collins to the Parsonage upon his return from Rosings is instantly attributed by Mrs Collins to the favour Elizabeth must have found in their eyes; and Darcy's calling unaccompanied some days later is enough to make her conclude that he is in love with her. His courtesy to the Gardiners in their first visit to Pemberley is instantly recognised by them – and by Elizabeth – as a superior compliment to their niece; and his driving his sister over to Lambton on the morning of her arrival is an attention to be accounted for by the whole party only in terms of affection for Elizabeth, Darcy himself having intended no less. These formal visitations speak loudly; but lesser signs can convey a great deal. Mrs Jennings's detecting love for Marianne Dashwood in Colonel Brandon 'from his listening so attentively while she sang to them' must be thought a better indication of Mrs Jennings's mind than of Colonel Brandon's. Emma Woodhouse, however, correctly takes a growing gentleness in Mr Elton towards herself and Harriet to mean an amatory design; and the looks which Darcy directs at Elizabeth, and Crawford bestows on Fanny Price, are marks of love. Fanny, having comprehended Crawford's behaviour towards Maria Bertram, is at a loss how to interpret these oeillades: 'in any other man at least, she would have said that it meant something very earnest, very pointed.'

Sir Thomas will probably not have observed these speaking looks; but he knows what Crawford has signified by a variety of attentions and emphases, and is to reproach Fanny with the fact that she 'must have been some time aware of a particularity in Mr Crawford's manners'. One of the unmistakable gestures has been his sitting down the moment Fanny does at the ball; in Miss Crawford's phrase, he was from then on 'devoted' to her. This is the understanding created when Frank Churchill, entering the Coles' drawing room, makes his way directly over to Miss Woodhouse, and declines to sit until he can find a seat by her. Emma divines 'what every body present must be thinking. She was his object, and every body must perceive it.' Much the same attention is accorded Elizabeth by Mr Collins. At Netherfield he continues perseveringly by her side, making it impossible for her to dance with others and rejecting her entreaties that he should find other partners. He professes an indifference to dancing; and lest appearances should fail of being plain, assures her that his object is 'by delicate attentions to recommend himself to her'. Though as heavy-footed here as in the dance itself, he knows how things are done.

It is on the basis of such intimations as these that Harriet Smith comes to Hartfield to give Emma the modest 'history of her hopes' of Mr Knightley. The signs of particularity are numerous. He has talked to her much more of late, with quite a different manner of kindness and sweetness. There have been expressions of approbation and praise. He has complimented her 'for being without art or affectation – for having simple, honest, generous, feelings'; commendations more direct, if anything, than those Captain Wentworth addresses to Louisa on the hill overlooking Winthrop. There are, too, the little details of the notice she has received from him which live in her memory and which she now recounts: 'a look, a speech, a removal from one chair to another, a compliment implied, a preference inferred' – things that have been unnoticed, because unsuspected, by Emma, but that for Harriet contain 'multiplied proofs'. The two strongest, which Emma is able to recollect, are Knightley's strolling apart with Harriet in the lime walk at Donwell – when he asked her in what seemed 'a very particular way indeed!' if her affections were engaged – and his having sat talking to her for half an hour during Emma's absence after saying he could not stay five minutes. His confessing at that time a reluctance to leaving home which he had not acknowledged to her gives Emma 'severe pain'. For Emma's reaction to this account, during which she realises her own love for Mr Knightley, is not to dismiss it as trifling, but to admit to Harriet and herself that it is decisive.

A marriage between these two will, she knows, be in every respect the 'most unequal of all connexions'; yet on the evidence presented to her she cannot but conclude that, 'She had brought evil on Harriet, on herself, and she too much feared, on Mr

Knightley.' From this conviction she proceeds to an achievement which is perhaps unique in the literature of romance. In the garden at Hartfield she silences, to his immense mortification, the man who has loved her through the years and is about to propose to her – in sheer terror lest he should speak only to tell her that he is going to marry her young protégée.

For a gentleman's advances need, and indeed can, only be slight – a fact which may as readily leave a lady uncertain of the meaning of his conduct as cause her entirely to misinterpret it. Anne Elliot is aware how conjectural her thought must be when she suggests to her friend Lady Russell that Mr Elliot's sudden desire for reconciliation with Sir Walter may be due, not to mere family considerations, but to her sister Elizabeth's being his object; for her sister is so consistently deferred to as lady of the house 'that any particularity of attention seemed almost impossible'. On the other hand, Captain Wentworth dreads that his immediate arrival after Louisa's engagement to Benwick is known, and his determined talking to Anne on this subject and on the past, have been all too weak as indications of his feelings. 'You alone have brought me to Bath,' he writes in frustration in his letter. 'For you alone I think and plan. – Have you not seen this? Can you fail to have understood my wishes?'

From tokens hardly less strong, Harriet understands wishes that are non-existent. Mr Knightley has acted honourably and in all innocence, but his behaviour has not been notably discreet, for the simple reason that the thought of his marrying Harriet can never have occurred to him. He has taken a kindly interest in her as a social inferior who happens to be the friend of Emma – who herself, with other predispositions, sees in his manner to Harriet a type of familiarity which must signify attachment. Ironically, through precisely the same cause she has been blind to similar tokens in Mr Elton's conduct towards herself, and blundered into a depth of indiscretion from which Mr Knightley, both as a man and as someone of immeasurably greater social consequence than Harriet, is preserved.

Mr Elton's advances have not been difficult to detect. So

pronounced have his sighings and languishings been that Emma thinks him, were this possible, almost too gallant to be in love; she is affected much as Elizabeth Bennet has been in the presence of Mr Collins, and at one stage has to run away to indulge the inclination to laugh at the sort of parade she finds in his speeches. Nonetheless she takes every opportunity to welcome him at Hartfield as Harriet's supposed suitor. Her brother-in-law's warning that Elton's goodwill is addressed to herself and that she should regulate her conduct accordingly alerts her at the moment when Mr Elton, emboldened by what he takes to be Miss Woodhouse's encouragement, embarks upon civilities more direct. At the Westons' dinner party he is addressing her with proprietary solicitude, anxious for her to be warm, entreating her not to visit Harriet's sick room once more, and appealing for Mrs Weston's support on the latter point with a tender, 'Judge between us. Have not I some right to complain?'

The question, amounting almost to a declaration, is not to be settled by Emma's look of reproach and her walking away. For – as he makes clear during his enraptured proposal in the darkness of the slow-moving coach – Mr Elton is professing sentiments which he is sure are already well known. Not that he has ever before had the chance to declare his 'ardent attachment and unequalled love and unexampled passion'; but his attentions have been such as cannot fail to communicate those feelings. Everything he has said or done in the past weeks, he tells the affronted heiress of Hartfield, has been with the sole view of marking his adoration. 'You cannot seriously doubt it. No! – (in an accent meant to be insinuating) – I am sure you have seen and understood me.'

Mr Collins's love for Elizabeth is as imaginary as Mr Elton's for Emma; his assurance is as unbounded. The latter fact may be ascribed to his greater vanity, since Elizabeth has been in no way as welcoming as Emma apparently has. Be this as it may, Mr Collins's emotions are no less fervent than those of his fellow clergyman: they even threaten at the start to run away with him, and their violence would have been expressed in the most animated terms, had not the subject of fortune mercifully supervened. But he, too, is addressing a lady he is sure has 'understood' him. His first observation, when Elizabeth has abandoned the thought of looking for refuge, is that she can hardly doubt the purport of his discourse. 'My attentions have been too marked to be mistaken,' he claims. 'Almost as soon as I entered the house I singled you out as the companion of my future life.'

We tell ourselves that Elizabeth has done nothing to merit these assurances; but Emma Woodhouse is unable to offer herself like consolation. Carried away by concern for Harriet's future, anxious to use every means to bring Mr Elton into her friend's company, she has relaxed the guardedness of her own behaviour, and suffered the consequence of unexpected and unwanted addresses. Once her indignation has abated, she is obliged to stop and admit that she has presented to Mr Elton manners 'so complaisant and obliging, so full of courtesy and attention' as to an ordinary and common understanding must appear as encouragement. No such error informs her conduct later on towards Frank Churchill: her actions here are as she intends them: she encourages an attitude of gallantry by permitting herself to seem pleased. Churchill, very correctly, takes the blame for what has happened in his voluminous letter of explanation. His behaviour has, he believes, indicated 'more than it ought'; but only the certainty of Emma's indifference to him prompted his over-distinguishing attentions. These she received, he writes, 'with an easy, friendly, goodhumoured playfulness' which exactly suited him. This impression was correct: as Emma confesses to Mr Knightley, 'my vanity was flattered, and I allowed his attentions.' Her well-deserved surprise in this second instance of unguardedness lies, not in the receiving of a proposal, but in the fact that one is not made.

Even if there were the slightest suspicion that Elizabeth Bennet might inadvertently have encouraged the first proposal made to her – a possibility which few would entertain – we are convinced that she can bear no shred of responsibility for the second. She has made her hostility to Darcy abundantly clear. Not for nothing is her astonishment beyond expression when, after perfunctory courtesies and an awkward silence, he comes towards her and with some agitation begins a declaration of love. The agitation soon disappears: while he speaks of apprehension, his look and manner show him confident of being accepted. His assurance might well derive in some degree from knowledge of the magnitude in material terms of what he is offering her: but can it be the whole reason? Can a man like Darcy be complacent at a moment like this purely upon the grounds of his personal gifts, his wealth, and his social eminence? If it were so, would he not be an insufferable poltroon? Yet how otherwise can we explain his behaviour, when we know that Elizabeth is so far from having tender feelings for him as to be positively antagonistic?

It would not be amiss, at the present point, to reflect upon what Mr Knightley has to say to Emma on the subject of Robert Martin's overture to Harriet Smith. It applies to affairs of the heart in general. Dismissing Emma's protestations on the social inequality of the young people, he affirms:

> 'Robert Martin would never have proceeded so far, if he had not felt persuaded of her not being disinclined to him. I know him well. He has too much real feeling to address any woman on the hap-hazard of selfish passion. And as to conceit, he is the farthest from it of any man I know. Depend upon it he had encouragement.'

Of the three motives here advanced for a man's proposing to a woman, we can rule out the first: Darcy is too much a man of feeling and principle to be impelled entirely by self-centred emotion. As for conceit, we know that he has it – he admits as much himself; but to account for his confidence by adding this motive to pride of possession would be to make him even more obnoxious. There remain only two possibilities: that Darcy has somehow conceived the notion of Elizabeth's 'not being disinclined to him' – a contingency not helped by the dislike she is not withheld from making evident; or that she has in some way unknown to herself contrived to give him encouragement. The first can invite conjecture only, but the second is open to investigation, since Elizabeth's speeches and actions are closely presented to us.

A hint, perhaps a clue, appears at the beginning of *Pride and Prejudice* in a word which, significantly, is also applied by Frank Churchill to Emma. Having rejected Elizabeth as a partner at the Meryton assembly because of her being not handsome enough to tempt him, Darcy afterwards becomes aware of her pleasing appearance. But more: though he recognises that her manners are not those of the fashionable world, 'he was caught by their easy playfulness.' A chance to sample them occurs during the party at Lucas Lodge. His coming near to listen to her conversation causes Elizabeth to try some impertinence, lest she should become intimidated; and at Charlotte's prompting she speaks to him in teasing fashion, demanding a compliment on what she has just said to Colonel Forster. Moments later, with an assumed gravity, she gives him the benefit of her thoughts on the 'fine old saying, which every body here is of course familiar with — "keep your breath to cool your porridge." '

This sportiveness seems innocent enough; but the element of mockery, or rather ridicule, that it contains makes itself increasingly evident. Elizabeth, indeed, is at her ease in the sardonic. At the Netherfield ball, vexed at Wickham's absence, she taunts Darcy while dancing with him with the idea of an arrangement to suit the dispositions of persons not wishing to be troubled with speech. At Rosings she enjoys herself and entertains Colonel Fitzwilliam by pestering Darcy with questions wittily directed at his diffidence in company, and scathing rejoinders to what he says in his own defence. The truism that practice makes perfect in social address as in music at last draws from him an ambiguous compliment on the playing she acknowledges to be deficient: 'You are perfectly right. You have employed your time much better. No one admitted to the privilege of hearing you, can think any thing wanting. We neither of us perform to strangers.' This is not the first indication he gives of ruffled feelings.

The conversation in fact has begun on a note of contention. Darcy, in coming up to the pianoforte, is met with the promise that his attempt to frighten Elizabeth by so appearing will fail. 'My courage always rises with every attempt to intimidate me,' she declares. A similar irascibility has been known at Netherfield Park, when, upon Caroline Bingley's playing a lively Scotch air, Darcy asks Elizabeth if she is inclined to dance a reel. She smiles but does not answer; and on being invited again, retorts that she will deny him the pleasure he is obviously seeking of despising her taste. 'I always delight in overthrowing those kind of schemes,' she informs him, 'and cheating a person of their premeditated contempt. I have therefore made up my mind to tell you, that I do not want to dance a reel at all – and now despise me if you dare.' The gallantry of his reply amazes her, for she had 'rather expected to affront him'. Elizabeth is assisted by that mixture of sweetness and archness in her manner which makes it difficult, as Jane Austen observes, for her to affront anybody. But the indignity is there. Allow for the effect of youth and beauty, remove Darcy's courtesy and state of 'bewitchment', and one is left with the fact of plain rudeness.

Not to her admirer alone is Elizabeth inclined to be belligerent. Her readiness to present her opinions with vigour, apparent in her first encounter with Lady Catherine de Bourgh, has been shown just as clearly if less memorably in the conversations at Netherfield, where an almost acrimonious pitch is once attained. Bingley's mild remark on the accomplishment all young ladies display stirs up a hornet's nest. Darcy's view of the rarity of true accomplishment moves Elizabeth to be no longer surprised at his knowing only six accomplished women, but to wonder at his knowing any; and his question at this seeming severity towards her own sex produces from her the indignant, '*I* never saw such a woman. *I* never saw such capacity, and taste, and application, and elegance, as you describe, united.' The immediate protest which arises from Bingley's sisters, and Caroline's bitter charge, upon Elizabeth's leaving the room, that she is one of those who try to gain favour with the other sex by undervaluing their own, do not show the depth of the injury: for in effect Elizabeth has scornfully denied their own accomplishment. Her adherence to truth – if what she says is true – or her contempt for the insincere, or for Darcy, causes such hurt to the susceptibilities of the ladies of the house as threatens to be socially disruptive.

Artifice and pretence are to Elizabeth Bennet's quick mind and enjoyment of the incongruous all too like the reek of gunpowder to a warhorse. Her celebrated reply to Caroline's praise of Darcy's impeccable character reveals her the embodiment of the comic spirit: 'Follies and nonsense, whims and inconsistencies *do* divert me, I own, and I laugh at them whenever I can.' That spirit, however, very readily incorporates the satirical, whose harshness is thereupon inflicted on Darcy himself. Provokingly, Elizabeth suggests to him that he is without such failings; and despite his qualified disclaimer she assures Caroline Bingley, who calls for the result of her 'examination', that this is so: 'I am perfectly convinced by it that Mr Darcy has no defect. He owns it himself without disguise.' Nor is she satisfied until she has with greater warmth accused him, on the strength of the self-analysis he has attempted, of 'a propensity to hate every body'.

This boldness in derision is always at its peak when Elizabeth is applying herself to the study of character. She prides herself on her perspicacity – but could lay claim to a frankness which even Lady Catherine might envy. Bingley's self-depreciation gives her as much scope as Darcy's complacency. His confessions of always deciding in haste and having a rapid flow of ideas gain from her tart responses – though she turns to defending him stoutly against Darcy's criticism. Concerning the latter's disposition she is less positive, as she admits to him during their dance at the Netherfield ball. The questions with which she plies him as to his manner of making judgments provoke at length puzzlement, and a caution not to carry on with her declared intention of sketching his character. Her persistence has the effect once more of disturbing him, as appears from the coldness of his, 'I would by no means suspend any pleasure of yours.'

The plea that she should desist from this pursuit had been voiced earlier by no less a person than Mrs Bennet, and in slightly more forceful a style. 'Lizzy,' she cries, upon her daughter's telling Bingley she understands his character perfectly, 'remember where you are, and do not run on in the wild manner that you are suffered to do at home.' The reprimand is pertinent, if demeaning: Elizabeth has indulged in a kind of behaviour which is in the strict sense unbeseeming and indiscreet. For once the maternal judgment has not erred. But time and again afterwards the roles are reversed: Elizabeth blushes at her mother's graceless sallies against the man whose slighting her daughter has so incensed her. Admittedly, the spirit of contention stalking abroad without the benison of wit wears an unlovely countenance; but Elizabeth's shame has little to do with the aesthetic. The querulous tones of, 'What is Mr Darcy to me, pray, that I should be afraid of him?' are a perspective into her own uncivil demeanour.

The comment Caroline Bingley vouchsafes to Darcy upon the woman who has so evidently charmed him is, as far as it goes, just and deserved. She advises him to check 'that little something, bordering on conceit and impertinence, which your lady possesses'. We admire Elizabeth for her liveliness, her wit, her sporting with inconsistencies, her naturalness and candour: but we shall err if through partiality we fail to see that she can be tempted by these qualities beyond the bounds of conduct proper for a young lady of her times. Her manner can be on occasion somewhat removed from gentility and refinement, particularly in her approach to men. In what Jane Austen calls her archness, and David Cecil terms her 'charming audacity',[1] there is a degree of freedom, of directness, and indeed of familiarity, which might appear as 'encouraging' in the eyes of the other sex.

What could be more interesting to a man than a young woman confronting him in the most spirited and lively style with home truths relating to himself – to his opinions and character? What, in that age of conformity of the sexes to conventions of restraint and reserve, can be more obviously 'particular'? The adverse nature of the lady's remarks might readily be understood on either side as a gesture to the requirements of modesty that was in effect a means of liberation from them. And would not their rigour tend to be mitigated, where the gentleman was concerned, by the 'mixture of sweetness and archness' in her manner which made it difficult for an Elizabeth Bennet to affront anybody?

Perhaps Elizabeth is too much of a person to be preoccupied with mere decorum, or for us to wish to confine her within the narrowness of codes and modes of her day. It may also be the author's conscious purpose to demonstrate, through comparison with a vibrant being of her own creation, the shabbiness and inadequacy of the system of comportment under which she lives: that human nature must be belied, if not thwarted, by its cramping categories. And the further moral might be implied that mutual hearts and keen minds can never be kept asunder by the prevailing social conformities, however rigid. Yet it remains true that by their standards Elizabeth is at fault. A lady she may be; but she is not invariably ladylike. This is by no means as unusual or anomalous a state as it sounds. It is considerably easier, if truth be told, to be a lady without being ladylike than it is to be a gentleman without being gentlemanly. And if the judgment seems harsh, Elizabeth herself is not unaware of her shortcoming.

She has known for some time that Darcy and she are ideally suited to each other: that while she must greatly benefit from his experience and soundness of judgment, his own mind might be softened and his manners improved by her 'ease and liveliness'. But when, in their conversation after his second proposal, Darcy gallantly takes responsibility for the disaster of the first, blaming his vanity for having led him to believe that she was desiring and expecting his addresses, she never doubts that this same liveliness has been the culprit. Instantly she replies, 'My manners must have been in fault, but not intentionally I assure you. I never meant to deceive you, but my spirits might often lead me wrong.'

Her woman's instinct will allow her no illusion about the effect of her conduct; and her curiosity and humour will give Darcy no rest until he, too, acknowledges it. Later, with spirits 'rising to playfulness again', Elizabeth commands him to account for his falling in love with her: 'what', she asks, 'could have set you off in the first place?' Advising him that her beauty, having been early withstood, is not to be held as cause, she goes on considerately to answer the question for him: 'my behaviour to *you* was at least always bordering on the uncivil, and I never spoke to you without rather wishing to give you pain than not. Now be sincere; did you admire me for my impertinence?'

His attempt to substitute the euphemism of liveliness of mind comes to naught. 'You may as well call it impertinence at once,' she declares. 'It was very little less.' We are apt to view this talk as Elizabeth's mettlesome jesting – but it contains the truth. The high-spiritedness which had broken through the palisades of custom; the impropriety which had allowed boldness to creep into her ways; even that union in Elizabeth of pleasantry and contention through which she had sought to express disapproval –

had all appeared to Darcy in the flattering guise of liking and invitation. She had imagined she was repelling him when all the while her indiscretions were giving him encouragement. She had done nothing less than put herself forward in sheer unguardedness. Darcy's proposal had been a surprise to herself: but upon the assumptions of her day it might have been predicted.

To think of adding Catherine Morland to the list of heroines unconsciously soliciting attentions from unwelcome suitors might be held critically suspect, on the grounds of taking someone like John Thorpe too seriously. That he takes himself seriously enough, and that Jane Austen devotes some attention to him, are scarcely arguments. But whatever we make of him, Catherine herself is important; and since the episode upon which her friend Isabella frames her accusation is as explicit as those between Darcy and Elizabeth or Mr Elton and Emma, it cannot be amiss to inquire into what is said.

The beginning is so unpropitious as to be almost the end. At Edgar's Buildings the gentleman comes into the parlour to announce that he is leaving, and the lady in as many words wishes him a good journey. His resort is to walk apart, hum a tune distractedly, burst into praise of 'this marrying scheme' upon which his sister has embarked, and ask Catherine what she thinks of the notion. Her delight at the engagement just confirmed by the arrival of Mr Morland's letter is expressed in the decided, 'I am sure I think it a very good one'; but to Thorpe, with head full of his new enterprise, the import of these simple words is very different. 'Do you?' he cries, brightening – 'that's honest, by heavens!' A reply thus inspiriting moves him to mention the old song, 'Going to one wedding brings on another' and suggest, with consciousness, that they might try its truth. If his accompanying laugh is foolish, the hint is clear – though it is lost on the pragmatic Catherine, who replies that she never sings.

Other advances receive the same treatment from a nature so artless and unsuspecting. He will come to pay his respects at

Fullerton; her mother and father will be glad to see him. He hopes that she will not be sorry to see him; there are few people she is sorry to see, and company is always cheerful. He thinks likewise, and their ideas appear pretty much alike on most matters; it may be, but she has never considered it. And so on. But when, in shy self-depreciation, she admits to not knowing her mind on many issues, the conversation strengthens. Thorpe is quick to relate her remarks to the subject of marriage: he also does not bother his brains with what does not concern him, he tells her, desiring no more than the girl he likes and a comfortable house over his head; and as to fortune, it is nothing. Catherine, still engrossed in her friend's happiness, finds interest in these words and readily agrees. 'Very true. I think like you there. If there is a good fortune on one side, there can be no occasion for any on the other. No matter which has it, so that there is enough.' But in a moment she is running off to spread the news of Isabella's engagement. Impatience and tedium may have helped force from her this measure of assent; but like sentiments stated so frankly on such a topic can, for Thorpe, have only one drift.

However this may be, there seems not enough in these replies to give him quite the resulting 'undivided consciousness of his own happy address and her explicit encouragement'. But their quality has been transformed by a single remark from Catherine as, eager to put an end to the discussion, she again wishes him a good journey, declaring she is to dine with Miss Tilney and must be going home. He detains her with, ' – Who knows when we may be together again? – Not but that I shall be down again by the end of a fortnight, and a devilish long fortnight it will appear to me.' Catherine's response, classic in brevity and moment, is made with delightful incomprehension.' ' "Then why do you stay away so long?" replied Catherine – finding that he waited for an answer.'

Her naive words are open to a startling interpretation: and Thorpe – with vanity to assist him – thereupon takes it. He is jerked into breathless commendation: 'That is kind of you, however – kind and good-natured. I shall not forget it in a hurry.' Then he burgeons even more falteringly into compliment. In making the assumption he does, and reading into every subsequent word of Catherine's a similar complaisance, he is scarcely at fault. Clumsily no doubt, but in the manner of that age, he has declared an affection; and Catherine, failing to recognise his meaning through her youth and inexperience, has with most expressive ambiguity appeared to accept it. If either is to be blamed, it must be she. Elizabeth Bennet is unguarded through some indifference to the modes of acquaintance and courtship; Catherine, through her immaturity.

Possibly because of dislike, but also certainly by instinct, Catherine is non-committal in almost everything she has said to John Thorpe, treating familiarity and praise with unconcern. Her behaviour is in accord with the claims of modesty as that age apprehends them; but it conforms, also, to a deeper understanding of the female character itself. A frigid reserve denotes a becoming chastity of demeanour; the masking of the feelings is requisite as a shield against casual and undesirable attentions; but it is even more important in countering forces from within – in saving a woman from herself. For it is in the very nature of her being that she is easily influenced: warmth of emotion and kindliness of disposition can readily make her a prey to masculine designs. She is vulnerable, because persuadable; and an attitude of frigidity – on the surface, at least – is her best weapon in her weakness.

Anne Elliot, less personally gifted than other of Jane Austen's heroines, is the most admirable in her womanliness. At the age of nineteen she is persuaded by Lady Russell to break off her engagement to Captain Wentworth. Eight years later she is almost persuaded by the same person to marry Mr Elliot – a possibility she can only admit to herself with a shudder of horror when, enlightened as to his character, she thinks of the misery which must have followed. No small part of the anguish Wentworth suffers on his appearance in Bath, in seeing Anne escorted by Mr Elliot and being aware of 'all the horrible eligibilities and proprieties of the match', is to know their union is desired by everyone who can influence her, to recall what persuasion had once done in the shape of Lady Russell sitting

behind Anne at the concert, and – even supposing the lady
reluctant or indifferent – 'to consider what powerful supports'
would be at Elliot's disposal to induce her into consent.

In this estimate Wentworth appears to be correct. Made
aware of his anxieties after all is happily settled between them,
Anne gently reproves him for not having allowed for the
difference in age, and the fact that her earlier action had been a
yielding to what she saw as an obligation to decide for safety in
the face of risk. But that evening, as they leave the card party and
stand together in apparent admiration of a display of green-
house plants, she voices a confession which confirms his
judgment. Upon reflection she believes that she was right to be
guided by Lady Russell, to whom she looked as a mother – right,
not in the outcome, but morally speaking. If she had ignored her
friend's importunity, she would have suffered in her conscience
the self-reproach from which she has been free; 'and if I mistake
not,' she adds calmly, 'a strong sense of duty is no bad part of a
woman's portion.' The same wisdom is implied in Mr Knightley's smiling condemnation of the newly wed Mrs Weston: she
is better as a wife than a governess, for in attempting to school
the wilful Miss Woodhouse she has received a very good
education from her, on the 'very material matrimonial point' of
submitting her own will and doing as she was bid.

It is not to self-regard alone, but to a confidence also that he
understands the natural responses of a woman in the heart of the
girl who faces him so reluctantly, that Henry Crawford's
assurance must be ascribed. He cannot doubt that such love as
his, in a man like himself, will if persevered in secure a return.
The terms in which he declares his affection cannot but impress
Fanny; for his feelings are genuine, and produce a marked
alteration in his manner. In this she finds claims which must
operate, rights which demand different treatment. 'She must be
courteous, she must be compassionate,' she tells herself; she
must have 'a sensation of being honoured'; and, whether
thinking of herself or her brother, she ought to be conscious of 'a
strong feeling of gratitude'. These promptings are not merely
evidence of Fanny's gentle character, but apply to womanliness
itself. They are present in Elizabeth Bennet, who at the height of
her indignation against Mr Darcy is distressed by her inability

to meet those needs which the situation and her own nature require. 'If I could *feel* gratitude,' she cries, 'I would now thank you.' The moment the injustice of her condemnation of him is fixed in her mind, and while resentment at his demeanour still rankles within her, tenderness establishes itself and 'his disappointed feelings became the object of compassion'.

The effect in Fanny Price of this feminine relenting, as Jane Austen describes it, is a manner so pitiful and agitated, as she tempers her refusal with words 'expressive of obligation and concern', that Crawford, vain, ardent and hopeful, cannot believe her indifferent. Indeed, says the author, he was not so irrational as Fanny thought him in the professions of 'persevering, assiduous, and not desponding attachment' which closed the interview. Had he not begun it in the state of being so delighted with the idea of making her love him within a very short time that he scarcely regretted her not loving him now? Sir Thomas Bertram himself is surprised when he learns next morning that an hour's entreaty from a young man like Crawford has 'worked so little change on a gentle tempered girl like Fanny'. And his son Edmund, despite knowing Fanny's dislike of Crawford's character and disgust at his amorous adventurism with Maria and Julia, does not think it possible that she can persist in her refusal. 'Well, though I may not be able to persuade you into different feelings,' he tells her near the close of their long discussion, 'you will be persuaded into them I trust.' To what degree his wishes regarding Mary Crawford affect him in this presumption must remain unknown; but it is reasonable to suppose that he is relying on the feminine amenability to persuasion in his own suit.

Like expectations of womankind affect the thoughts of Mr Collins in declining to take his dismission from Elizabeth Bennet. There is no reason – apart from what may lie in the genius of comedy – why what in him is found to be an absurd persistence should be regarded in Crawford as no more than a somewhat admirable stubbornness. On Elizabeth's thanking him for the honour of his proposals but stating that she is unable to do other than decline them, Mr Collins obligingly gives her and us chapter and verse for his sanguine expectations. With a formal wave of the hand he assures her of his acquaintance with the custom among ladies of refusing, perhaps more than once, the man whose offer they secretly mean to accept. He is therefore by no means discouraged by what she has just said, and will hope to lead her to the altar ere long. The fact that Elizabeth's increasing exasperation cannot impress his urbane certainty is no doubt due more to knowledge of her financial situation than understanding of feminine psychology; nonetheless, his belief that when sanctioned by the 'express authority' of both her excellent parents his proposals cannot fail to be accepted by her, is genuine. It is true that Elizabeth dismisses him in silent contempt for 'such perseverance in wilful self-deception'. But he is no more guilty in this than Crawford, and is deserving of credit for unfailing good temper when assailed in a style the timid Fanny Price could not begin to imitate. In their confidence that 'the true delicacy of the female character' which has prompted the lady to decline their hand will allow her to be persuaded into accepting it, there is nothing to choose between the two men.

To do her justice, Fanny does not shrink from the task when obliged to confront Henry Crawford. Though mildly, she speaks her thoughts, advising him that she does not, cannot, shall never love him, urging that the subject is painful and not to be renewed, and specifying, when pressed, dispositions which by nature, education and habit are so incompatible as to make mutual affection impossible. Her pleas are ignored, her arguments disputed; there is no way in which she can counter this determination. What hope is there of Fanny succeeding, when an Elizabeth Bennet fails? In her negatives Elizabeth is rather more economical: instead of reasonings, she presents Mr Collins with the stark, 'You could not make *me* happy, and I am convinced that I am the last woman in the world who would make *you* so' – adding however with a touch of inspiration her certainty of Lady Catherine's disapproval. But even against this direst of apprehensions Mr Collins is proof; and though Elizabeth gets to the point of insult, the diatribe of, 'My feelings in every respect forbid it. Can I speak plainer?' produces only the awkward gallantry of his, 'You are uniformly charming!'

Not to the impassioned admirer alone, but to society at large, is the idea of a woman's refusing the proposal of an eligible and prepossessing man almost beyond belief. Sir Thomas Bertram, true enough, is a little set in his ways; but his atttitude, if in harmony with most of the conventions, is that of an acute and questioning mind. His reaction when, after an unaccustomed ascent to Fanny's fireless room, he hears her deny Crawford's report of having been given encouragement, and assert her intention never to give it, is steeped in a Lear-like incredulity.

> 'Am I to understand,' said Sir Thomas, after a few moments silence, 'that you intend to *refuse* Mr Crawford?'
> 'Yes, Sir.'
> 'Refuse him?'
> 'Yes, Sir.'
> 'Refuse Mr Crawford! Upon what plea? For what reason?'
> 'I – I cannot like him, Sir, well enough to marry him.'
> 'This is very strange!' said Sir Thomas, in a voice of calm displeasure. 'There is something in this which my comprehension does not reach.'

Crawford is not only a man of position and fortune, but the possessor of notable qualities of mind and agreeableness of disposition; he has been some time acquainted with the Bertram family; his sister is Fanny's intimate friend; and his affection is strong and disinterested. In the face of these facts, which Sir Thomas with remorseless logic sets before her, Fanny's response is unaccountable.

The Grants and Edmund, as well as Crawford and his sister, share this feeling of near-disbelief. Edmund informs Fanny that the surprise at the Parsonage 'seems to have been unbounded. That you could refuse such a man as Henry Crawford, seems more than they can understand.' No more comprehensible to Mrs Ferrars and the circle of her acquaintance than Edward's declining to marry Miss Morton, daughter of Lord Morton, with thirty thousand pounds, is the idea that Miss Morton might decline to marry either of the brothers. Elinor is amused, when calling at Harley-street, to be told by John Dashwood that they are thinking of Robert Ferrars's marrying Miss Morton instead. By way of reply she supposes, coolly, that the lady has no choice in the affair. John is puzzled; and on her re-phrasing her inquiry to presume it must be the same to Miss Morton whether she marry Edward or Robert, she is assured, 'Certainly, there can be no difference; for Robert will now to all intents and purposes be considered as the eldest son; – and as to any thing else, they are both very agreeable young men, I do not know that one is superior to the other.' Elinor, we learn, says no more.

That a woman should have feelings which determine choice, and the right as a human being to exercise it, is by no means undisputed in the world Jane Austen sets before us. Society's materialism, and the role for women which it decrees, indicate a subjection. The certainty of a Mr Collins that his dear cousin's refusal of his addresses 'is merely words of course' has more solid basis than vanity alone. His self-flattering conviction is supported by the prevailing outlook in many respects, not least upon the question of the amount of latitude a young woman should enjoy. For, quite apart from the principle of freedom to choose, parental pressures and obligation to family must influence her wishes. The mindless Mary Musgrove states the generally accepted position in her banal objection to the marriage her husband foresees between Henrietta and Charles Hayter. 'I do not think any young woman has a right', she declares, 'to make a choice that may be disagreeable and inconvenient to the *principal* part of her family, and be giving bad connections to those who have not been used to them.' As always, Mary is consulting her own preferences; but in the concept itself she is attuned to the thinking of her age.

It is from the lips of Fanny Price, the gentlest and most sensitive of her heroines, that Jane Austen makes her most powerful plea for women's feelings to be accorded dignity and respect by a society which, for all its fine sentiments, spurns them in its practice. When Edmund Bertram tells her, affectionately, that she must repair the impression made on Mrs Grant and Mary by her rejection of Crawford – 'prove yourself to be in your senses as soon as you can, by a different conduct' – Fanny makes a speech untypical in its contentiousness, which ranks with Anne Elliot's words on woman's constancy:

> 'I *should* have thought,' said Fanny, after a pause of recollection and exertion, 'that every woman must have felt the possibility of a man's not being approved, not being loved by some one of her sex, at least, let him be ever so generally agreeable. Let him have all the perfections in the world, I think it ought not to be set down as certain, that a man must be acceptable to every woman he may happen to like himself.'

But even if this were so, and Crawford had every imaginable quality and claim, how could she be expected to greet overtures from him with feelings answerable to her own, and be in love with him the moment she was asked – especially in view of her social position? 'We think very differently of the nature of women,' she concludes, 'if they can imagine a woman so very soon capable of returning an affection as this seems to imply.'

This weary rebuke in defence of true womanhood is directed to the inhabitants of the Parsonage, but meant no less for the man Fanny loves. But it will not reach the person who gave origin to her thinking. Fanny has tried without success to influence her uncle; she must henceforward speak instead by what she is: always the best form of reasoning but the slowest of communication. When he began his interrogation as to the cause of her declining Crawford's proposal, she knew she had failed. 'She had hoped', comments the author, 'that to a man like her uncle, so discerning, so honourable, so good, the simple acknowledgement of settled *dislike* on her side, would have been sufficient. To her infinite grief she found it was not.' It becomes quickly evident that it is not her motive but herself that is under attack. Her character is the very reverse of what Sir Thomas had imagined: wilful, perverse, and permeated with 'that independence of spirit, which prevails so much in modern days, even in young women'. She has acted, he tells her, without consideration for those who have surely some right to guide her, not so much as asking their advice; and the question of the advantage or otherwise of the match to her own family she has disregarded – despite her awareness of the immense benefit to them such an establishment for her would bring. She has thought selfishly, incited by 'what a young, heated fancy imagines to be necessary for happiness', and dismissed an opportunity of being settled in life – 'eligibly, honourably, nobly settled' – which would probably never occur again. Another eighteen years might go by, Sir Thomas warns, in tones that recall those of Mr Collins, without her being addressed by a man of half Mr Crawford's estate, or a tenth part of his merits. If one of his own daughters had declined such a marriage, he would have thought it 'a gross violation of duty and respect'. Fanny does not owe him the duty of a child; but can her own heart (he demands, through her sobbing) acquit her of ingratitude? In thus presuming, as a young woman, to choose for herself in the matter of attachment and marriage, Fanny Price may properly appear, in the eyes of the most benevolent and moral of beings, as a repository of the marble-hearted fiend.

Sir Thomas is unwontedly moved by Fanny's grief at these charges. He hears with surprise and disappointment that she has remained firm in her refusal during the hour-long interview with Crawford that follows at his insistence; but he decides to let things proceed without further interference from himself, hoping instead that the course of time and a lover's importunity 'might work their usual effect'. Only when he is trying to reassure Fanny later on, after she has ventured once more to explain her feelings, do we hear from him the graciousness in self-contradiction of, 'You will have nothing to fear, or to be agitated about. You cannot suppose me capable of trying to persuade you to marry against your inclinations.'

The evidence, however, is much in favour of this supposition, both as regards Sir Thomas and society as a whole. Young women could readily be prevailed upon, in their allotted position, to follow the accepted line of duty to parental wish and family interest. In the minds of many of Jane Austen's contemporaries it was axiomatic that to be a woman is to be tractable, upon issues of varying degree of moment. Catherine Morland's steadfastness in wishing to keep her engagement with the Tilneys next day despite their entreaties that she should accompany them to Clifton is vexation to the Thorpes, but also revelation to her brother. 'I did not think you had been so obstinate, Catherine,' he tells her; 'you were not used to be so hard to persuade; you were once the kindest, best-tempered of my sisters.' So far is James from being mollified by the answer that she hopes she is not less so now but must do what she believes to be right, that when she runs off to try to undo the harm of John Thorpe's truthless message, he withholds Thorpe from following after her with the angry, 'Let her go, let her go, if she will go. She is as obstinate as − '[2] The simile, which, Jane Austen adds, would if finished have been an improper one, he feels to have been amply merited by the heroine's unnatural tenacity of purpose.

In much the same way does Edmund Bertram react to the more substantial matter of Fanny's wanting nothing to do with Henry Crawford. She had thought that, like his father, Edmund blamed her for her refusal; but she hears from him soothing sentiments when he comes to speak to her about it. How could she have imagined him an advocate of marriage without love? Even if he held no strong view on that topic, he is greatly concerned for her happiness. Sorry or surprised he may be at what he has heard; but, he tells her, 'I think you perfectly right.' The matter does not admit of a question: 'You did not love him − nothing could have justified your accepting him.' Fanny, we are told at this point, 'had not felt so comfortable for days and days.' But the tune insidiously changes. Though Fanny's conduct has so far been faultless, Crawford, with no common degree of attachment, hopes in time to create in her that regard which she does not possess now. 'Let him succeed at last, Fanny, let him succeed at last,' Edmund urges, with an affectionate smile: 'You have proved yourself upright and disinterested, prove yourself grateful and tender-hearted; and then you will be the perfect model of a woman, which I have always believed you born for.' Fanny's reply is the vehement, 'Oh! never, never, never; he never will succeed with me.' She blushes instantly at so indecorous a degree of emphasis; and Edmund, 'quite astonished', reproaches her with a dismayed, 'Never, Fanny, so very determined and positive! This is not like yourself, your rational self.' Such inflexibility in a lady, where the declared love of an eligible suitor is concerned, can, even in the eyes of a sympathetic young man of her own times, be none other than abandonment of proper conduct.

In traditional terms, it is 'cruelty'. Edmund does not so accuse her; but the inference is plain in what follows. Her suitor, he declares, has been too hasty, not allowing for her youthful fondness for Mansfield; had Henry been guided by his plans he believes that, between them, they should have won her. But steady affection will bring Crawford his reward: 'I cannot suppose that you have not the *wish* to love him – the natural wish of gratitude. You must have some feeling of that sort. You must be sorry for your own indifference.' In other words, a woman who is not by her nature prompted to a warmth of compliance and yielding in the face of unexceptionable proposals is cruel.

The case is put in jocular style but with serious intent by Mrs Smith to her friend Anne, who has affirmed her intention of not marrying Mr Elliot despite all popular anticipation. 'How I do wish I knew what you were at!' she exclaims. 'I have a great idea that you do not design to be cruel, when the right moment comes. Till it does come, you know, we women never mean to have any body. It is a thing of course among us, that every man is refused – till he offers. But why should you be cruel? Let me plead for my – present friend I cannot call him – but for my former friend. Where can you look for a more suitable match? Where could you expect a more gentlemanlike, agreeable man?'

The same convictions respecting himself and the caprice of women sway the mind of Mr Collins upon his apprising Elizabeth Bennet that, in view of its being the established custom of her sex to reject a man on the first application, he is far from accusing her of cruelty at present. Our finding his statement absurd – as, in its context, it can be no less – is no doubt helped by the term's being metaphorical, in common usage and in song. But the preconceptions with regard both to her femininity and her situation with which he hastens to encounter Elizabeth show Mr Collins to be at one with the common expectations of the day.

And more violently, perhaps, than anyone else in the novels is he to be affected by them.

In the society to which he belongs, where the regulation of

manners produces reserve of conduct and repression of feelings, the slightest indications of regard or favour must make a considerable impression – as an Emma Woodhouse or a Captain Wentworth will have good cause to remember. When we observe what may befall Jane Austen's heroines through their inadvertence, we might well wonder what a female – admittedly, of less heroic stature – might not achieve through conscious purpose! This is a subject, obviously, which will never be much spoken about; but fortunately John Dashwood has no reserve, as he has no doubts, upon the matter. Believing Colonel Brandon to be in love with Elinor, though for a number of reasons undecided whether to proceed, he assures his sister that a very little trouble on her side will secure him – that 'some of those little attentions and encouragements which ladies can so easily give, will fix him, in spite of himself'. The advice is kindly meant, but addressed in the wrong quarter; certainly it is materialistic and crude; but it is far from being unsound, nonetheless. Woman might be assigned a subordinate status, subjected to social pressures and prohibitions, and looked on as a creature fit only for humility and submissiveness; but the very limitations of her role give her a corresponding power of no mean sort.

The consequence of a merely pleasant and obliging manner towards Mr Elton has been unmistakable. In her subsequent reflections, though, Emma does not take account of a much more positive feature of her behaviour in his presence. Abstracted through concern for her protégée, she has made statements intended for Harriet's benefit which can easily be understood to imply something quite different – to be, in fact, precisely some of those 'little attentions and encouragements' which John Dashwood has in mind. One is in her words to Mr Elton on the charade – ostensibly by his friend – which she has written into Miss Smith's collection. He must take her apologies to this gentleman, she advises, as he looks doubtingly. 'So good a charade must not be confined to one or two. He may be sure of every woman's approbation while he writes with such gallantry.' The effect upon Elton of this fearless compliment from a lady is dramatic; it can be compared only to John Thorpe's reaction to Catherine's asking him why, if absence will be so tedious, he does not return sooner.

> 'I have no hesitation in saying,' replied Mr Elton, though
> hesitating a good deal while he spoke, 'I have no hesitation in
> saying – at least if my friend feels at all as *I* do – I have not the
> smallest doubt that, could he see this little effusion honoured as *I*
> see it, (looking at the book again, and replacing it on the table,) he
> would consider it as the proudest moment of his life.'

Emma is highly diverted by this pretentious and stumbling
speech – not knowing that it comes from a man who, as he has
reason to think, has just received an avowal of affection.

But her other unwitting token is one of so much more tender
regard that he makes no speech at all; he looks, Jane Austen
says, 'as if he did not very well know what answer to make;
which was exactly the case'. Emma meets him a few yards from
Miss Goddard's, where Harriet lies ill, and tries to discourage
him on the invalid's account from attending the Westons'
dinner party that evening. She must go, because her father has
decided to: 'But, upon my word, Mr Elton, in your case, I should
certainly excuse myself. You appear to me a little hoarse
already, and when you consider what demand of voice and
what fatigues to-morrow will bring, I think it would be no more
than common prudence to stay at home and take care of
yourself to-night.' After this amiable exhortation she walks on,
while he mutters acknowledgment of its being very cold. She
thinks she has achieved her object, 'too eager and busy in her
own previous conceptions and views', the author points out, 'to
hear him impartially, or see him with clear vision'. As for Elton,
Jane Austen adds, with disarming brevity, that he is 'very much
gratified by the kind care of such a fair lady'. His proposing to
the fair lady in the coach on the way back from the Westons' is
not quite the piece of presumption Emma thinks it is. He does
not in truth merit her anger at his claim that she has given him
encouragement.

Nor, if the signs are correctly interpreted, is Mr Collins as
presumptuous in proposing to Elizabeth Bennet as she thinks he
is. Although he changes from Jane to her on the first morning of
his stay at Longbourn, his interest does not become in any way
obtrusive until the occasion of the ball at Netherfield. A reason

might be found in what has happened upon the invitation's being received. Elizabeth is in such high spirits as to break her own rule of not speaking to him unnecessarily. Laughing to herself, she asks the solemn young man if he will be at the ball, and whether he considers it will be proper for him to join in the evening's amusement. She finds, we are informed, that he will venture to dance without scruple or fear of rebuke, either from the Archbishop or Lady Catherine de Bourgh; but also, to her chagrin, that her liveliness has never been worse timed. 'I am so far from objecting to dancing myself,' Mr Collins continues, 'that I shall hope to be honoured with the hands of all my fair cousins in the course of the evening, and I take this opportunity of soliciting yours, Miss Elizabeth, for the two first dances especially.' As always, his speech is ceremonious; his action in gravely asking her to partner him is in the circumstances a piece of necessary civility; but his view of Elizabeth's inquiry and its motive will be unlike her own. For her, he has merely been the unfortunate means of converting her feelings from amusement to vexation. But can we doubt that he will see in her question an anxiety that he should be at the ball, and an intimation of her favour? If the ordinary patterns of conduct will not lead him to place this interpretation on her imprudence, his vanity assuredly will. His confidence in requesting her hand in marriage may owe not a little to what Elizabeth has unknowingly conveyed.

But in a far greater sense is Mr Collins victim rather than criminal, patient rather than agent. For the full panoply of feminine power is soon preparing its onslaught at Netherfield Park, as Charlotte Lucas obligingly diverts some of his now marked attentions from her friend. With the might and craft, not of innocent error but of conscious and culpable intent, Charlotte has determined to secure her friend from any return of Mr Collins's addresses by engaging them towards herself. She puts her scheme into effect with near-military method and resolution. By the end of their next social encounter at the Bennets' dinner party appearances are favourable for her. What is comprised in Jane Austen's remark that Charlotte had been 'tolerably encouraging' is left to the reader's imagination; but it certainly bears out John Dashwood's advice to Elinor as to how a woman can fix a man in spite of himself. For it nerves Mr

Collins, despite the diffidence caused by the adventure of the Wednesday, to steal out of Longbourn House on Friday morning and throw himself at the feet of his newly beloved, who, having discerned his manoeuvre from her post of observation at an upper window of Lucas Lodge, has already advanced in force, armed to withstand both love and eloquence, to intercept him accidentally in the lane. The shrewdly conducted campaign is over almost before it has begun, the objective gained with ludicrous ease.

The completeness of Mr Collins's overthrow, at the hands of the second of the two women to whom he has proposed within three days, is of course a comment on his character: he cannot be a man of any depth of feeling. But it is also an instance of the hazardous conditions under which the courtships of that age are conducted. The social round's routine civilities, during courtesy visits, dinner parties and occasional balls, offer few opportunities for true contact – as Elizabeth Bennet has emphasised to Charlotte on Jane's behalf. The code of proper behaviour for the sexes limits whatever encounter there is. Meetings between a man and woman attracted to each other are likely to be brief and constrained, though emotionally charged: not well suited to the forming of sound judgment and mutual understanding, but calculated to lead to uncertainty, misapprehension and error in the approach to one's prospective partner, or in the choice itself. They minister quite readily to what Sir Thomas Bertram terms a heated fancy. Mrs Gardiner deprecates Elizabeth's use of the expression 'violently in love' to describe the state of Bingley's affections, as being often applied to feelings arising from a mere half-hour's acquaintance; and when Elizabeth instances his growing inattention to other people in his preoccupation with Jane, her aunt somewhat contemptuously finds it a symptom 'of that kind of love which I suppose him to have felt.' But Bingley himself is ready so to accept it. According to Darcy, he believed Jane to have a regard for him which was sincere, if not equal to his own, and would probably have proposed to her despite his sisters' device of going to London and the remonstrance there made, had it not been for the assurance which Darcy gave of Jane's indifference. This plea admittedly acted on a person of great modesty and dependence on his friend's judgment; but that it should succeed shows the difficulty confronting young people of reaching confidence as to the other's disposition and feelings, and their own.

Something of the nature of the hindrances can be gleaned from Elizabeth's assuming, on being called to her father's library, that the letter from Mr Collins which he has before him is an application from Mr Darcy for her hand. As the colour rushes into her cheeks, she is not certain whether she should be pleased at Darcy's having explained himself at all, or offended that the letter was not addressed to herself; but however she chose to respond, the very formal method of declaration would have been perfectly usual, and causes no surprise. According to such modes Mr Collins is not quite as ridiculous as we like to think him in apologising to Mrs Bennet for having addressed Elizabeth on the subject of marriage 'without having paid yourself and Mr Bennet the compliment of requesting you to interpose your authority in my behalf', and for accepting his dismission from their daughter's lips instead of their own. However, we can have little sympathy for the stiffness of manner and resentful silence he subsequently displays; he has been injured in pride only, since his regard was imaginary. In his pique he can be compared to Mr Elton, whose state of mind, in the 'long, civil, ceremonious note' he sends so unwontedly to Mr Woodhouse, with its pointed exclusion of his daughter's name, could not have been made more plain. To take a more charitable view of their umbrage, though, would be to see them as suffering from the hurt to which emotional error and self-deception could give rise within the system they knew.

But women, from their secluded position, are the greater sufferers. The shelter society affords them is also a snare: the significance it attaches to manner makes them easy prey to dissimulation. Anne Elliot looks upon the cousin she meets at Camden-place as 'without any question their pleasantest acquaintance in Bath; she saw nobody equal to him'. The strong but regulated family loyalties he displays; the unostentatious liberality of his style of living; that due regard for public opinion which does not preclude independent judgment; the moderateness of disposition which is yet receptive to the simple and the lovely – all these add to the impression of his manners which has been the first recommendation. The regard which Mr Elliot feels for her creates in Anne 'agreeable sensations' – as Lady Russell intends it should. The assertion that they 'should not suit', forced from her by her friend's enticements, arises from a sense that she still does not really know his character after a month's acquaintance. What is apparent to her she cannot fault, though some emerging hints of former ways are not in keeping; but the nub of the matter is that, rational, discreet, polished as he is, he is not open. The love of Captain Wentworth has been for her an education both liberal and liberating. 'Her early impressions were incurable. She prized the frank, the open-hearted, the eager character beyond all others. Warmth and enthusiasm did captivate her still.' Anne Elliot is saved by one of life's chances. Nothing otherwise in her upbringing and experience could have dimmed her cousin's attractiveness in her eyes, or lessened the 'great deal of good will towards him' she has consciously felt. The later revelation that he is 'black at heart, hollow and black!' would have been a tragic one.

The same fate would have overtaken Elizabeth Bennet if it had not been for her poverty. Wickham, she confides to Mrs Gardiner, is for her 'beyond all comparison, the most agreeable man I ever saw' – an estimate her aunt concurs in. The charges against him in Mr Darcy's letter bring, first resentment, then consternation. Elizabeth realises not only that she knows practically nothing about Wickham, but that, had the means of gaining knowledge been available to her, she would never have felt a wish to inquire: 'His countenance, voice, and manner, had established him at once in the possession of every virtue.' By no means had such prepossession about Mr Elton been able to establish itself in the fastidious mind of Emma Woodhouse; but she had not for a moment doubted his good nature, and finds it 'dreadfully mortifying' when he proves himself 'in many respects, the very reverse of what she had meant and believed him; proud, assuming, conceited; very full of his own claims, and little concerned about the feelings of others'.

Making mistakes about people is endemic to the human condition; and in any age, to take to oneself a spouse is in the nature of a calculated risk. But society's operation as Jane Austen saw and understood it contrived in some ways to deepen the inherent perils. She would never have accepted Charlotte Lucas's philosophy that 'Happiness in marriage is entirely a matter of chance': that, since compatibility of the parties is no guarantee of happiness in view of divisions time will produce, it is better to have as little prior knowledge as possible of the person you are to marry. The author is one who knows a *non sequitur* when she comes upon it. Nor would she approve the cynicism of Mary Crawford which will have it that 'there is not one in a hundred of either sex, who is not taken in when they marry'. But that impression of life which has caused Mary to find on all sides people deceived as to the qualities of their partner and having to put up with 'exactly the reverse' of what they had expected must, to some extent, be a reflection of Jane Austen's own experience. For her novels of romance and courtship present a formidable array of unsuitable and unfortunate matches – a fact which is almost certainly a comment upon the assumptions, manners and methods of her times.

And we cannot but be grateful to her, for it is highly diverting. What, we find her asking herself, has made a man like Mr Allen select a woman like Mrs Allen for his mate? She belongs to 'that numerous class of females, whose society can raise no other emotion than surprise at there being any men in the world who could like them well enough to marry them'. Beauty, genius, accomplishment, even manner, she is without. Only the air of a gentlewoman, passive good temper and a trifling turn of mind can account for the choice of a sensible, intelligent man like Mr Allen. Having made the mistake, he is at all times intent on reducing its significance: he allows his wife's observations to flow unimpeded when he is in her company, and uses his best endeavours to place himself out of it. His leaving her and Catherine Morland to 'enjoy a mob by themselves' in their first visit to the Upper Rooms in Bath proves the rule of his subsequent behaviour. Sir John Middleton is perhaps more fortunate in his wife's having no observations to make. Not that his are worth hearing: contrasted as these two people are, they in fact are alike in that blankness of mind which confines him to the role of sportsman and his lady to that of a mother, and produces a union of the boisterously senseless with the glacially insipid.

In publicly faulting the manners of his mother-in-law Mrs Jennings, Mr Palmer brings upon himself the reproach of his wife. Laughingly as always, she endearingly accuses him, 'My love, you contradict every body. Do you know that you are quite rude?' With reciprocal tenderness he replies, 'I did not know that I contradicted any body in calling your mother ill-bred.' Mrs Jennings proclaims the fact that, abuse her as he may, he has taken her daughter out of her hands and cannot give her back again; Charlotte Palmer laughs at her husband's predicament, and exultingly declares she does not care how cross he is to her, as they must live together. Elinor Dashwood, after a little observation, decides that Mr Palmer likes to appear more ill-natured than he is, and concludes in revealing style:

> His temper might perhaps be a little soured by finding, like many others of his sex, that through some unaccountable bias in favour of beauty, he was the husband of a very silly woman, – but she knew that this kind of blunder was too common for any sensible man to be lastingly hurt by it.

Mr Palmer is the type, as well as the prototype, of Elizabeth's father. Mr Bennet, sardonic and withdrawn, has acquired through the years that wisdom which allows him to be indebted to Mrs Bennet only as her ignorance and folly contribute to his amusement. This, says the author succinctly, is not the sort of happiness which a man would in general wish to owe to his wife: 'but where other powers of entertainment are wanting, the true philosopher will derive benefit from such as are given.' The grimness of this state of things, reflected in the terse wording, has been appreciated to the full by Mr Bennet's second daughter. Had her opinions all been drawn from her own family, we are told, Elizabeth 'could not have formed a very pleasing picture of conjugal felicity or domestic comfort.'

To types of consolation and expedience not dissimilar have wives been driven by their husbands' deficiencies. According to her son, General Tilney's lady, though genuinely valued by her martial consort, was often distressed by his behaviour. 'He loved her,' Henry informs Catherine, 'I am persuaded, as well as it was possible for him to – We have not all, you know, the same tenderness of disposition – and I will not pretend to say that while she lived, she might not often have had much to bear.' Enough has been said – certainly to make his ensuing re-proaches to Catherine at her suspicions about his father seem slightly less charitable than they might be. As for the deceased Lady Elliot, who for seventeen years had had the awesome task of humouring, softening or concealing Sir Walter's failings and promoting his respectability, one must think she receives but slender tribute in the observation that she had been 'an excellent woman, sensible and amiable; whose judgment and conduct, if they might be pardoned the youthful indiscretion which made her Lady Elliot, had never required indulgence afterwards'. Veneration rather than praise would seem here to have been more appropriate.

The afflictions of Mrs Grant, of Mansfield Parsonage, are not small if her sister is to be believed. Mary Crawford sees Dr Grant as an indolent, selfish bon-vivant who, if the cook makes a blunder, is out of humour with his excellent wife. An explosion of wrath 'about a green goose, which he could not get the better of' having indeed contributed to driving her and Henry from the house, Edmund is forced to concede the fact of wifely suffering, and intimate to Fanny that they cannot defend the clerical husband. But through her experience, Mrs Grant attains a higher if bleaker philosophical plane than Mr Bennet. She makes a spirited defence of the married state against Mary's somewhat warm allegations. Too much is apt to be expected of it, and little rubs and disappointments there will be: 'but then, if one scheme of happiness fails, human nature turns to another; if the first calculation is wrong, we make a second better; we find comfort somewhere.' Her argument is reason itself – but it would be more impressive if the force with which it is put did not introduce a note of desperation. Not for nothing does Mary mockingly honour her sister's *esprit de corps*.

If these be the chief examples of infelicitous wedlock, there are clouds of supporting testimony. We never meet the Reverend Mr Norris, but knowledge of his dear lady may drive us

128

to apprehension as to his temporal comforts. Nor are we introduced to Admiral Crawford, uncle and guardian of Mary and Henry. He and his late wife, it is revealed, were united in affection for these children, 'though agreeing in nothing else'. More than one reason is suggested by his conduct after her death. Fanny Price's sojourn at her parents' house in Portsmouth enables us to draw our own conclusions as to the suitability of their marriage; and the whole of her residence in Mansfield invites us to do the same concerning her uncle and aunt. By what irony of fate or sport of destiny is someone of Sir Thomas's personality and powers of mind bound to a woman engaged interminably upon useless and inelegant pieces of needlework, thinking more of her pug than her children, though indulgent to the latter so long as it does not put her to inconvenience, and needing to be guided by others in all matters? Their daughter Maria's marriage to Mr Rushworth is just as monumental a mishap; and Julia's elopement with the Honourable John Yates has nothing to do with affection, or even respect. After her disappointment over Henry Crawford she had allowed Yates's attentions with very little idea of accepting him; and if Maria's scandalous conduct had not increased her dread of home and the severity and restraint that must await her there, he would probably never have succeeded. 'She had not', the author trenchantly remarks, 'eloped with any worse feelings than those of selfish alarm. It had appeared to her the only thing to be done. Maria's guilt had induced Julia's folly.' That *Mansfield Park* is not the most cheerful of the novels is largely due to its being a kind of matrimonial mausoleum.

But evidence of conjugal calamity, presumptive or apparent, is before us wherever we look. What chance can there be for Mrs Elton's *caro sposo*? Will Harriet Smith, under the care of Robert Martin, be as likely to be led aright and turn out very well as Mr Knightley anticipates, despite the 'little wit' with which he has at first credited her? We naturally hope so – but have greater confidence regarding Jane Fairfax and Frank Churchill, whose union is favoured not only by the glow of romance, but by her principle and his inherited ease of disposition. Theirs will not end up like that of his adoptive parents at Enscombe, the alliance of an ineffectual George with a veritable dragon. Such a conclusion might well threaten the connubial bliss of Lucy Steele and the vainglorious Robert Ferrars, though: for the harmony in which they settled down to their life together was typified by 'the frequent domestic disagreements' between them. From any like gladiatorial involvement their mother had been released by the wise expiry of Mr Ferrars. And as much has to be said with respect to Lady Catherine de Bourgh. We are given sufficient grounds for supposing her character to have been as celebrated for its sincerity and frankness in the time of Sir Lewis as it is latterly, and for deducing therefrom that any marriage to which she was party must have encroached upon the calamitous. The course charted by the barque of true love in Jane Austen's novels is one positively bestrewn with drifting wrecks – to say nothing of the reefs of convention and decorum upon which the frail vessel may so promptly founder.

As has been seen in such instances as Elizabeth Bennet's finding favour in Mr Darcy's eyes, Mr Elton's aspiring to the hand of Emma Woodhouse, and Charlotte Lucas's appropriation of her friend's hapless suitor, the social rigidities which normally retard attachment can in certain situations serve to precipitate it. Mr Collins is not the only man to propose to two women in a very short time. Admittedly, the space of three days is more glorious than the four weeks it takes Mr Elton to meet upon the rebound, court and become betrothed to Miss Augusta Hawkins of Bristol, if not Bath; but the tale of his gaining her 'with such delightful rapidity' captivates the newsmongers of Highbury, the lady having been so easily impressed, so sweetly disposed, and, says the author, 'to use a most intelligible phrase, been so very ready to have him'. However, it does not follow that a quick courtship need have anything tawdry about it – as that delightful couple, Admiral and Mrs Croft, demonstrate. Anne Elliot knows no better example of happiness in marriage. But they met under the exigencies of national crisis, as the Admiral explains in deploring the unconscionable length of time Captain Wentworth is taking to choose between the two Musgrove girls. 'If it were war, now,' he declares, while steering his gig erratically in the direction of Kellynch 'he would have settled it long ago. – We sailors, Miss

Elliot, cannot afford to make long courtships in time of war.'
His question as to how many days it was between their meeting
and their sitting down together in their lodgings in North
Yarmouth is discreetly parried by Mrs Croft, who remarks
pleasantly that their friend, hearing how soon an understanding
was reached, would never be persuaded that they could be
happy together. When she affirms, 'I had known you by
character, however, long before,' her husband responds with,
'Well, and I had heard of you as a very pretty girl; and what were
we to wait for besides? – I do not like having such things so long
in hand.' War or no war, one is led to think, Admiral Croft
would have been nothing if not brisk.

But had not Mr Collins heard of Jane and Elizabeth Bennet as
very pretty girls? He has scarcely been seated in Longbourn
House before he is complimenting Mrs Bennet on her family of
beauteous daughters – to very good purpose. In planning his
visit he has had a wife in view: 'he meant to chuse one of the
daughters, if he found them as handsome and amiable as they
were represented by common report.' He is spurred on not only
by inclination, but by his patroness's particular advice; and is
not Lady Catherine's express wish, for Mr Collins, the equiva-
lent of military necessity for Admiral Croft? Certainly in his
situation, and the brief interval of parish duties available to him,
Mr Collins, too, cannot afford to make long courtships. But in
his powers of decision he is unparagoned. His switch from Jane
to Elizabeth is accomplished with a celerity which puts Admiral
Croft in the shade. It is done while Mrs Bennet is stirring the fire.

Speed is not an indispensable feature of romance. To the extent
that it is often seen as an enhancement, however, Mr Collins has
made some small contribution to legend, whatever he is and
does besides; and when his amorous quests are viewed together
with those of the other men in the novels, it is clear that, if he be
at all an offender against romance, he is not by any means alone
in meriting opprobrium. But to speak of romance in Jane
Austen's world is something of a misnomer. Hers are rather
stories of attachment and marriage. The power of emotional

attraction and romantic love is fully appreciated: but it is only one amongst a number of considerations within the process of courtship – and far from being the chief.

The closest the writer ever comes to romance's praise is in the situation of the forlorn Anne Elliot, who has been forced into prudence in her youth, and learns romance as she grows older, 'the natural sequel of an unnatural beginning'. Yet, though she tells herself she would never give to any young person the counsel upon which she formerly acted, she remains convinced of having done the right thing in submitting to the prudential arguments and seniority of Lady Russell. At the novel's end Jane Austen speaks her concluding word on the subject. When any two young people take it into their heads to marry, they are pretty sure by perseverance to carry their point, however poor, imprudent or deceived in each other they may be. 'This,' she says, 'may be bad morality to conclude with, but I believe it to be truth.' The fact she alludes to is never in doubt; but the morality to which it appears to stand in such bold defiance is of the greatest interest.

To act solely upon romantic motive is to set at naught the understanding of marriage that predominates in the novels: to scorn the authority of society, of caste, of family, and of finance. The older generation tends to pay mere lip service to the idea of love in marriage – but so do many of the young, if an Edmund Bertram is at all representative. William Price is of a different spirit. While lamenting from his heart that his sister should be so cold towards Henry Crawford, he is, the author explains, 'of an age to be all for love, and therefore unable to blame'. Such sentiment is the mark of immaturity. To this degree is Emma Woodhouse in error in the expectations fostered for Harriet Smith; but she makes no similar mistake in her personal attitude to marriage. And at the report of Jane Fairfax's self-reproach for agreeing to a secret engagement she displays a composedly pitying manner. 'Poor girl!' she says to Mrs Weston. 'She loves him, then, excessively, I suppose. It must have been from attachment only, that she could be led to form the engagement. Her affection must have overpowered her judgment.' This is the simple condition of error – of a falling from grace – in any young woman, as Jane herself readily admits.

The pathos and the unwisdom of reliance upon strong affection is shown in the career of Marianne Dashwood. No love like that she has felt for Willoughby can ever come to her again; but her salvation is brought about through feelings of quite another kind. They are induced by the 'confederacy' of her mother, sister and brother-in-law united in promoting the suit of Colonel Brandon, by the knowledge of his goodness, and by realisation at last of his devotedness. She does not love her mature, flannel-waistcoated admirer; but in the situation which reveals itself, as the author asks, what could she do? 'Instead of falling a sacrifice to an irresistible passion, as once she had fondly flattered herself with expecting', she overcomes her former affection and gives her hand, voluntarily, to a man she has considered too old for marriage, 'with no sentiment superior to strong esteem and lively friendship'.

The modern critic may see her fate as disastrous for all that is amiable and gladsome in the relation of man and woman, and in the mind of Jane Austen. But though she doubtless found something to regret in it (it is there, in two small words, when she tells us that Marianne's heart became in time as much devoted to her husband as it had once been to Willoughby) she leaves us in no doubt, not only of the happiness of the marriage, but of the triumph of rectitude which it represents. For in her understanding, romantic passion is not the best, or even a good, basis for settlement in marriage. She would have agreed with Sir Thomas Bertram, who, despite being impressed by the strength of attachment Fanny Price has created in Crawford, can by no means approve of 'the transient, varying, unsteady nature of love, as it generally exists', from whose effect she so far seems immune. Sir Thomas is blamed nonetheless for his reasoning with regard to Maria's betrothal. From her careless and cold demeanour to Mr Rushworth he has known that Maria does not like him; and advantageous as the alliance would be, he is ready to sacrifice it for the sake of his daughter's happiness. But, influenced by the social and material benefits to be gained, he permits Maria's peremptory assurances to get the better of his discernment. He tells himself that Mr Rushworth is young and will improve, and that if his daughter can speak so confidently of her future with him uninduced by 'the prejudice, the blindness of love', she ought to be believed; that 'A well-disposed young woman, who did not marry for love' would be the more attached to her own family, and thereby have access to a fund of 'the most amiable and innocent enjoyments' for the gladdening of married life. These are not Sir Thomas's true thoughts, but rather the distortions to which the prospect of acquisitions for his house gives rise, and which make him happy to adduce whatever ideas about Maria's disposition are suitable to the purpose.

But though he allows them too much weight, the considerations are real; and in his taking them into account, and readiness to use his authority either to forbid or, as in this case, to encourage a match, he is acting as a father should. For the parental role is to ensure that the objective calculations requisite to a settlement take place. Sir Thomas would have found an ideal daughter in Elizabeth Bennet. Fired by the romantic as she is in her attraction to Wickham, she can remain aware of the claims of the prudential. She knows the dangers of the lack of fortune; and to her aunt's advice that she must not let her fancy run away with her, but use the sense she is known to possess, she replies simply and conventionally, 'I see the imprudence of it.' As a young woman in love, or in a state of great liking, she reminds Mrs Gardiner that where there is affection, the immediate want of fortune seldom prevents young people becoming engaged; but she accepts the advice she is given, to the extent of undertaking not to be in a hurry. 'When I am in company with him,' she promises, 'I will not be wishing. In short, I will do my best.' When Wickham, yielding to the charm of a suddenly acquired ten thousand pounds, forsakes her in favour of Miss King, Elizabeth has no fault to find in his wish for independence. On the contrary, nothing, she tells herself, could be more natural; it is 'a wise and desirable measure for both'. Her heart has fortunately been but slightly touched, and vanity is appeased by the reflection that she would have been Wickham's only choice, had fortune permitted it. She resents her aunt's later suggestion that Wickham is mercenary. What, she demands, is the difference in matrimonial affairs between a suitor's mercenary course, and the prudent motive upon which a young woman might reject him? and as for any indelicacy in

Wickham's swift change of sentiment, a man in distressed circumstances 'has not time for all those elegant decorums which other people may observe.' Nonetheless, in this attitude, as Jane Austen is concerned to point out, Elizabeth is 'less clear-sighted perhaps in his [Wickham's] case than in Charlotte's'. Why, indeed, must the woman be condemned to the disabling prerogative of finer feelings?

Charlotte Lucas has liberated herself from this condition, in accepting Mr Collins 'solely from the pure and disinterested desire of an establishment'. The author's irony reinforces her heroine's indignation at this conduct. Elizabeth had appreciated that her friend's views on matrimony were different from her own, but she had never supposed it possible that she would so act on them as to have 'sacrificed every better feeling to worldly advantage'. By taking the prudential to its logical conclusion, she has, in Elizabeth's eyes, conducted herself indelicately. Aware of this, Charlotte makes the defence she knows will not convince: 'I am not romantic you know. I never was.' She asks only a comfortable home; and considering her future husband's character, connections, and situation in life, she believes her chance of happiness with him to be 'as fair, as most people can boast on entering the marriage state'. This reasoning, Elizabeth, as she tells her sister, finds inconsistent, and in every way unaccountable. But that it would carry conviction, and win approval, in society generally is evident from the nature of Jane's mild but earnest response:

'You do not make allowance enough for difference of situation and temper. Consider Mr Collins's respectability, and Charlotte's prudent, steady character. Remember that she is one of a large family; that as to fortune, it is a most eligible match.'

Her plea that Charlotte might have something like regard for their cousin falls on deaf ears. Mr Collins being what he is, Elizabeth retorts, Jane must feel, as she does, that the woman who marries him cannot have a proper way of thinking. Jane's words are however a corrective, not only to her sister's vivacious argument, but to the thoughts of those modern readers who, like Elizabeth, can see nothing but inappropriateness and absurdity in an attachment where Mr Collins is one of the partners, and where love is not present.

For Charlotte and Mr Collins, unknown to themselves, obtain a kind of revenge. The romance which we conclude has no part in their relationship never really enters into the relationship between Elizabeth and Darcy which the novel sets forth. Even though attracted to him, Elizabeth cannot tell herself she loves him; her thinking remains on a prudential level. Before setting out with the Gardiners to wait on Miss Darcy at Pemberley, she examines her state of mind. She respects, esteems, is grateful to Mr Darcy; she feels a real interest in his welfare; she only wants to know 'how far she wished that welfare to depend upon herself', and how far it would be for the happiness of both that it should. Her question is answered, not during the visit, but in the few minutes when she is alone after the news of Lydia's elopement has been revealed to him. At that poignant moment she knows she would rejoice in the continuance of an acquaintance which now seems to have reached its end. The author at this stage chooses to enter the story and present her own judgment upon the heart of her liveliest heroine.

> If gratitude and esteem are good foundations of affection, Elizabeth's change of sentiment will be neither improbable nor faulty. But if otherwise, if the regard springing from such sources is unreasonable or unnatural, in comparison of what is so often described as arising on a first interview with its object, and even before two words have been exchanged, nothing can be said in her defence, except that she had given somewhat of a trial to the latter method, in her partiality for Wickham, and that its ill-success might perhaps authorise her to seek the other less interesting mode of attachment.

The basis of the affection Elizabeth comes to feel for Darcy is the same kind of regard for known qualities, and esteem for constant devotion, which leads Marianne Dashwood to accept Colonel Brandon – with a grain added of such receptiveness to considerations material as, even amidst nobler promptings, cannot efface the impression of her first seeing Darcy's beautiful grounds at Pemberley. She can indeed assure her father she loves him; but her path has not been by way of the romantic, but by 'the other less interesting mode of attachment'. In the purely prudential, Charlotte outdoes her: for Elizabeth entertains for her man that true respect which Mr Bennet so desired she should, and which Charlotte, knowing that in her situation it cannot be forthcoming, has made up her mind to dispense with. But Mr Collins, when he proposed to Elizabeth, could never have imagined he was viewed with anything other than the highest approbation; and had this and his own fancied affection for her been facts, we should not feel that the concept of attachment and matrimony with which he is armed in paying his addresses to her is markedly dissimilar to her own.

Marriage in Jane Austen's world, says David Cecil, 'was not regarded as a culmination of a romance but as a social arrangement for the promotion and maintenance of the family'.[3] As an institution of primary importance it was to be held in honour, and its ordinances upheld and defended. Nowhere, except in praising the imperious civility of Lady Catherine de Bourgh, does Mr Collins express himself more forcefully than upon the ill-consequences, as he sees them, of Lydia Bennet's escapade. And it is upon this topic that he may be thought to appear at his very worst – to show the cloven hoof, in adopting a manner which is reprehensibly high-handed and severe. Parsonical zeal runs away with him, in other words, and transforms him into a bigot. In a letter provoked by news of the elopement, and supported by the full authority of Lady Catherine, he comforts Mr Bennet with the assurance that the death of his daughter would in comparison have been a blessing, and urges him, in the choicest prose, to throw off his unworthy child from his affection for ever, and leave her to reap the fruits of her own heinous offence.

But this is a subject on which Mr Collins is not the only one to speak categorically. Nothing can be more severe – or more touching – than Jane Fairfax's self-condemnation for what, in her own eyes, is the crime she has committed against stringent and even sacred standards in consenting to a secret engagement. The suffering her action has brought her she accepts as a just

desert; but it cannot expunge her guilt. 'After all the punish-
ment that misconduct can bring,' she tells Mrs Weston, 'it is
still not less misconduct. Pain is no expiation. I never can be
blameless.' The morality of the Bennet family may be judged a
trifle less elevated than this; but the shock of Lydia's behaviour
and its implications unites them all behind Mrs Bennet's
strident urging to Mr Gardiner to '*make* them marry'. Elizabeth
is aghast at the fate they are willing upon Lydia; her reaction
when a marriage settlement is known to be possible is to cry,
'And they *must* marry! Yet he is *such* a man!' Her father's briefly
confirming that there is nothing else to be done cannot still her
wonder at their being forced to rejoice and be thankful for her
sister's predictable unhappiness in being united to an acknowledged scoundrel. But in a short time social constrainings have
re-exerted themselves; and though Elizabeth can see little better
than misery as being in store for her sister, 'in looking back to
what they had feared, only two hours ago, she felt all the
advantages of what they had gained.'

The Bertrams are less fortunate. The scandal and infamy
which the Bennets had apprehended in Lydia and Wickham's
living together without the sanction of marriage descends on
them through Maria's leaving her husband and eloping with
Henry Crawford. Upon this infamous proceeding all save Mary
Crawford and Mrs Norris think alike, though the positions
taken are characteristically diversified. Mr Price, reading of it in
his newspaper in the glare of the evening sun, intimates to Fanny
that 'there's the devil to pay' among her fine relations, and in
unkempt indignation swears, 'by G –, if she belonged to me, I'd
give her the rope's end as long as I could stand over her.' Fanny
spends a night entirely sleepless, passing from feelings of
sickness to shudders of horror, from hot fits of fever to cold; but
her mental condition is more afflicting. The incident itself seems
'too horrible a confusion of guilt, too gross a complication of
evil' to have been enacted. She can scarcely see how Sir Thomas
and Edmund, with their honourableness and integrity of mind,
and ties of kinship, can 'support life and reason under such
disgrace'; and she is led to feel that instant annihilation would,
in terms of this world alone, be the greatest blessing to everyone
connected with Mrs Rushworth.

Fanny Price, it is known, is of extremely timorous and impressionable disposition; and we might expect a more blessed insensibility from Lady Bertram. Fanny attends her, on her return to Mansfield, with customary kindness and sympathy – but in no other way can her aunt be comforted. Her reflections are not profound, but, says Jane Austen, guided by Sir Thomas she thinks justly on all important points: 'and she saw, therefore, in all its enormity, what had happened, and neither endeavoured herself, nor required Fanny to advise her, to think little of guilt and infamy.' She is in fact able to expect no outcome other than 'the loss of a daughter, and a disgrace never to be wiped off'. Edmund's affliction must be greater: his grief includes loss of the woman he loves, and suffering of a different order at the moral turpitude she shows in regarding in terms of expediency only 'the dreadful crime committed by her brother and my sister'.

His father's feelings are not explored until, upon Maria's separation from Crawford, the question of her accommodation arises. Sir Thomas will not hear Mrs Norris's entreaty that Maria be received at home; and on her angrily blaming Fanny as his motive, assures her that had there been no young person at Mansfield to be endangered by Mrs Rushworth's society, he would never offer 'so great an insult to the neighbourhood, as to expect it to notice her'. He will ensure her comfort and protection as his daughter;

> but farther than *that*, he would not go. Maria had destroyed her own character, and he would not by a vain attempt to restore what never could be restored, be affording his sanction to vice, or in seeking to lessen its disgrace, be anywise accessory to introducing such misery in another man's family, as he had known himself.

He voices the sentiment of society at large. The inhabitants of Longbourn and Meryton would have expected no other course from the Bennet family had Lydia's disgrace not been averted by the guilty pair's being persuaded into wedlock. News of the settlement is accepted with 'decent philosophy' in their neighbourhood. It would have been more to the advantage of conversation, according to the author, if Lydia had come upon the town, 'or, as the happiest alternative, been secluded from the world, in some distant farm house' – in the kind of establishment, 'remote and private', to which Maria is ultimately consigned, in Mrs Norris's care.

As it is, Lydia is restored to respectability. Shameless herself, however, she remains the cause of shame to her kin; and it is touch and go whether she will be received at Longbourn House. In a manner almost identical to Sir Thomas's own, her father announces to the exultant Mrs Bennet, who has been going through a list of possible residences for the newly-weds, 'Into *one* house in this neighbourhood, they shall never have admittance. I will not encourage the impudence of either, by receiving them at Longbourn.' Their request for such measure of recognition meets at first an 'absolute negative'; but he cannot long hold out against Elizabeth's and Jane's persuasion – and the fact that a marriage has been accomplished, and society's demand satisfied. In the words Sir Thomas applies to his other daughter, Julia, and John Yates following their elopement and marriage, the erring couple are in the end pardonable as having been guilty of folly rather than vice.

But only just! When Mr Bennet summons Elizabeth to his room to hear the final letter of Mr Collins, he can make up for his failure to divert her at its presaging her nuptials with Darcy, by laughing at his cousin's recommendation that he should forgive Lydia and Wickham as a Christian, but never admit them in his sight or allow their names to be mentioned in his hearing. '*That*', cries Mr Bennet, 'is his notion of christian forgiveness!' He might well laugh – for the notion has almost been his own. Mr Collins's moral theology may be seen as wayward; but there can be no doubt that in taking this position he is expressing convictions and feelings widely present in the minds of contemporaries where the defence of marriage is at issue. For it was held as an institution to be created out of the things by which society itself was composed – the formal, the material, the personal and the spiritual; and to contemn or defy its ordinances could be understood as doing none other than to pose a threat to the social fabric.

Here as elsewhere, Mr Collins is fulfilling a particular role. In all his actions he must give rise to amusement. But whatever he is engaged in, be it offering dutiful subservience to Lady Catherine de Bourgh, composing compliments for her and for ladies in general, impressing Elizabeth Bennet with the slightness of her prospects of marriage, responding to Charlotte's encouragement, or reproving Mr Bennet for admitting Lydia to his house, he is bringing into prominence the manners and practices of the society of which he forms part. The maladriotness of the man always exposes the usages – and shortcomings – of a system.

8

Dearth

If Mr Collins is in many ways a representative figure, why is he so sharply distinguished from other characters as an object of amusement? The answer lies of course in his foolishness; but one must be ready here to meet any Polonius-like objection to the attempt to define true folly – for there is plenty of method in evidence. Mr Collins's fault can in fact be seen as taking the ways of his world rather too seriously: founding his own thinking so thoroughly upon them, or using them so largely as a substitute for thought, as to leave little scope for real awareness or individuality. His career may thus be looked upon as a study, diverting, as all such studies must be, in small-mindedness – of the deadly effect of literalism. For he conducts himself according to the letter rather than in the spirit of his times.

Mr Collins's presence can be a trifle wearisome, as persons as diverse as Mr Bennet and Mrs Collins quickly discover; and one might well be tempted to view him in the light of Mr Elliot's definition of good company as being constituted by birth, education and manners, and at a pinch dispensing with education. The rule has its stringencies, and would certainly disqualify Mr Collins; but is it very much of a guide? A veritable mountain of noble nurture has been in labour only to bring forth the mouse of a Lady Dalrymple; and the author of the maxim which would admit him to the elect is himself more than a little of a rogue. In estimating any of the characters one surely cannot do better than apply those universal standards of virtue, sense and taste to which, according to David Cecil, each of them is inflexibly related by the author.[1]

Good sense, the eighteenth century's prime canon of excellence, does not excite us – but it can affect one of Jane Austen's heroines quite otherwise. Having perceived Colonel Brandon to be a man so possessed, Elinor Dashwood compos lly assures the disparaging Marianne and Willoughby, 'sense will always have attractions for me.' To Anne Elliot it is as much a gratification, on meeting him for the first time, to know that the future owner of Kellynch is undoubtedly a gentleman having an air of good sense, as it is to learn later that she has won his approval. The inelegance and confusion of her parents' house in Portsmouth impels Fanny Price to a new appreciation of her home at Mansfield Park. True, warmth of family affection is not much to be found there; but 'If tenderness could ever be supposed wanting,' she muses, 'good sense and good breeding supplied its place.' So sovereign is this attribute that one touch of it, seemingly, can make the whole world congenial.

In the characters of Colonel Brandon and William Walter Elliot, we are given to understand what is comprised in it. Sense denotes first a thorough knowledge of life, and intelligence of a high degree. The Colonel is a man of considerable experience, reads widely, and has 'a thinking mind'; Mr Elliot likewise displays knowledge of the world, a good understanding, and a discretion which, while respecting the set ways of common thought, is not governed by them. Both are men of polished and engaging manners suffused with apparent kindliness, Brandon in particular, as Elinor observes, being 'on every occasion mindful of the feelings of others'. Elliot exhibits in good measure the temperateness and restraint which is, perhaps, the distinguishing outward property of sense: he is 'steady, observant, moderate, candid'; yet there lives, beneath this self-possession, a discernment more sensitive and profound than that known in characters readily moved to enthusiasm.

The presence of sense is very quickly recognisable. Lady Middleton's habitual reserve soon reveals itself to Elinor as 'a mere calmness of manner with which sense had nothing to do'; whereas a few minutes of Mr Elliot's company, when he calls in Camden-place at ten o'clock on the first evening of her stay, is sufficient to create certainty in Anne. 'His tone, his expression, his choice of subject, his knowing where to stop, – it was all the operation of a sensible, discerning mind.' The same test appertains to Robert Martin's letter of proposal to Harriet Smith. From its vigour and clarity of thought and accomplishment of expression, and the moderation which informs yet does not detract from its delicacy of feeling, Emma cannot avoid recognising the work of 'a sensible man'. The affirmative sign, in a word, is that of a constant and felicitous judgment. Whether it shows itself in small things or great, it is its own recommendation; but it is most surely to be prized at those moments when it counters the assault of the emotions: when an Elizabeth Bennet can employ its force against every inclination in the matter of an imprudent marriage to Wickham, or at the point where her sister Jane, convinced that Bingley now has no thought of her, exerts command over grief for her family's sake and her own, and achieves that inner harmony which a poet might name 'the nobler fortitude/Of patience and heroic martyrdom/Unsung'. Certain it is that when Jane Austen describes Mr Knightley as a sensible man of about seven or eight and thirty, she has said a great deal.

Quite as much is conveyed when, in answer to his daughter's question as to whether the writer of the letter of self-invitation to Longbourn House can be a sensible man, Mr Bennet replies, simply, 'No, my dear; I think not.' Its extraordinary deference to Lady Catherine de Bourgh shows a subservience; the kind intention of christening, marrying, and burying his parishioners whenever it were required, an officiousness; its pomposity of phrasing, a self-importance; the apologising for being next in the entail, an irrelevance, which are all manifestly in conflict with sound judgment. The letter warns Mr Bennet, and the reader, that there never will be found in Mr Collins the union of discernment, moderation and sensibility which makes possible a consummately realised selfhood.

But good sense is no more than a supreme kind of competence in dissociation from that endowment with which it is generally seen as being conjoined. Colonel Brandon has won Elinor's esteem; but the validating concept in her approving description of him is surely the last: 'a sensible man, well-bred, well-informed, of gentle address, and I believe possessing an amiable heart'. Similarly, what recommends Mr Elliot to Anne upon further acquaintance is the thought that 'a warm heart' underlies the agreeable manners which are presented to her. The heart's disposition for Jane Austen is the source of goodness in a human being. She requires the persons of her novels to live virtuously, as David Cecil puts it – to be charitable, honest, disinterested, faithful, and so on.[2] But the category of virtue is rather too wide for the present purpose. It can include the negative rectitude of a Lady Middleton, the oppressive innocence of a Miss Bates – and, without doubt, the well-doing, such as it is, of Mr Collins, who, whatever might be said of him as a cleric, is as a man worthily-inclined and respectable. Further, someone like Sir Thomas Bertram may be looked up to as the pattern of virtue, and yet be grievously in error and the cause of irreparable harm. Morally speaking, what passes for virtue in the social setting may be no more than a manner, a custom, or an adherence to precept – and, in being no more, a death-in-life. For the life or soul of virtuous conduct is the heart's prompting.

Mr John Dashwood, we are told at the beginning of *Sense and Sensibility*, is not an ill-disposed young man, 'unless to be rather cold hearted, and rather selfish, is to be ill-disposed'. The development of his character illustrates that process, God-like in its dispassionateness and comprehension, of the author's love for the person, good or bad, whom his own imagination has brought into existence. Flourishing like the green bay tree amidst events (apart from the setback of his supplication to his enraged spouse on Lucy Steele's behalf), Dashwood is suffering all the time in bark and bole the effects of advancing blight and vitiation, and excites a type of revulsion which can never arise from the contemplation of Mr Collins. But his amiable sister Elinor has 'an excellent heart'. Her disposition is affectionate and her feelings are strong, though she exhibits a self-command denied to her mother and despised by her sister; it is the warmth of her nature that endears her to us despite the slight priggishness bestowed on her for the purposes of a didactic novel. With more true delicacy than Marianne she is better able to appraise the vulgarity of Mrs Jennings: the incorrectness and unfeelingness which gives her sister pain she has always sensed to be superficial. Yet she can resist, on cogent grounds, Marianne's eagerness to accept that lady's invitation to them to stay with her in London. 'Though I think very well of Mrs Jenning's heart,' she says to their mother, 'she is not a woman whose society can afford us pleasure, or whose protection will give us consequence.' The story shows the creation of an unlikely, even an impossible friendship, forged by Mrs Jennings's passionate defence of Edward Ferrars's constancy, and a depth of grief and 'kindness of heart' during Marianne's illness which 'made Elinor really love her'. As with the mother, so with the daughter: the 'openness and heartiness' of Mrs Palmer's conduct more than atones, in Elinor's mind, for her unrelieved silliness and frequent deficiencies in the forms of politeness.

Good and virtuous behaviour is the cement of society; but Elinor, for all her correctness of attitude, is able through this more intimate awareness to reach out in sympathy to one whose defiance of its forms has not only earned its condemnation but injured the sister who is very dear to her. She has nothing but indignation and contempt for Willoughby when he appears out of the night, summoned by remorse, to know if Marianne is alive or dead. By the time their conversation is at an end she has forgiven and pitied him, wished him well, felt an interest in his happiness, and realised the influence of his personality upon her own – for, she declares, he has proved his heart 'less wicked, much less wicked' than she had believed it. From Willoughby's puzzlement and anger at his past dealings, his wonder in looking back at his treatment of Marianne that, as he puts it, 'my heart should have been so insensible', Elinor knows that his is a redeemable nature. In her reaction she is not unlike the young Fanny Price, when, lonely and estranged in the mansion to which she has been transplanted, she comes to learn that her cousin Edmund's heart is warm and his temper affectionate. From then onwards Mansfield is home to her, and life meaningful.

Very different is the response of Anne Elliot to a similar intimation, upon finding herself being assisted into the Crofts' carriage by Captain Wentworth as the walking party is resuming its way back to Uppercross. She understands his action. He has not forgiven her for the past; he is perfectly indifferent to her, while becoming attached to another woman – but he cannot be unfeeling in the knowledge of her fatigue. She knows it is a mere remainder of former sentiment, an impulse of pure friendship, and no more. But as 'a proof of his own warm and amiable heart', the gesture induces such heightened and conflicting emotions as must distract her mind for a while from what is going on around her.

As he talks later with Anne at the White Hart about the devotedness of man to woman, Captain Harville, trying vainly to describe the experience of being reunited with dear ones after years of peril and separation, resorts with rare fervour to the heart's own language. Concerned at the position into which argument might seem to have driven her, Anne is at pains to declare the absolute value which 'the warm and faithful feelings' of any fellow mortal hold for her. Each is oppressed with thoughts of an undying affection; and each is aware of being challenged to the very utmost of creaturely sensibility. What is in question is nothing less than the sacrificing love: something which goes beyond common goodness, yet without which any goodness remaining in the human condition would be dubious indeed. They speak of the principle which is at once the source of virtue, the bond of persons and the touchstone of souls; of a rightness in human beings that becomes a righteousness as self is left behind. This benign power active in man is, for Jane Austen, not restricted to romantic attachment in which it is more evident, but appropriate and vital in all aspects of living; and to be without qualities of heart is to fail of attaining stature, to be in a real though not obvious sense a cripple, or even a monstrosity.

Life amongst mankind, as she appreciated, affords many such instances of moral catastrophe; with sympathetic insight she ensures that her novels do likewise; and Mr Collins, blissful in his ignorance, is one of the examples.

Bad taste is adherence to things inferior – the ignorant forsaking of the good in order to batten upon the spectacular and meretricious. It is, appropriately enough, the predisposition of Milton's Mammon, wherever providence places him:

> for ev'n in heav'n his looks and thoughts
> Were always downward bent, admiring more
> The riches of Heav'ns pavement, trod'n Gold,
> Than aught divine or holy else enjoy'd
> In vision beatific.

What is most admirable, in spiritual and temporal realms alike, has to do not with accidentals, but with whatever can give fulfilment through possessing true significance. In his concern with the trappings and externalities of existence, his veneration of size and splendour, Mr Collins is of course sadly astray. Tastelessness characterises his dealings with people throughout, from the first utterance regarding the handsomeness of the Bennet girls to his last address to their father upon the management of his domestic affairs. This conduct, happily, stands in no need of comment, but speaks for itself; nevertheless, a comparison between Mr Collins and others in this respect can be revealing – for he is scarcely alone.

Perhaps the most serious instance of bad taste in the novels is Henry Crawford's emphasis in speaking of Thornton Lacey. He is less concerned with what his friend Bertram is to devote himself to than with the house he will live in when he is doing it. The property has his qualified approval: anyone might suppose, looking at it, that it had been the demesne of a respectable country family for a couple of centuries, and is now the residence of persons spending two or three thousand a year. But he wants it to be improved so as to acquire 'such an air as to make its owner be set down as the great land-holder of the parish, by every creature travelling the road'. He is not averse, naturally, to these creatures being impressed by stately sermons of literary quality. No more would General Tilney be; but the General's dearer concern as resident landholder is apparently that he should himself be constantly impressed by the glories of his dwelling. His showing his guest Catherine over Northanger Abbey is a chance for him to indulge this wish. When they enter the magnificent drawing room, he makes good the limited commendation Catherine is able to offer by himself supplying all the minuteness of praise, and 'satisfied his own curiosity, in a close examination of every well-known ornament'; and in the dining room he cannot forego the pleasure of pacing out the length, for Miss Morland's more certain information.

The same worthy predilection is to be seen in Mr Collins – or perhaps one more worthy, since his rapturous air as he points out to his visitors from Longbourn the fine proportions and finished ornaments of the entrance hall at Rosings, or enumerates the windows in front of the house, or relates what the glazing 'altogether had originally cost Sir Lewis De Bourgh', is excited by the possessions of others. There is in fact no discernible difference when he draws their attention to the merits of his own humble abode. The party is delayed only by his praising the neatness of the Parsonage's entrance, and is called on to admire every article in the room, from the sideboard to the fender. The vistas from the garden are similarly presented for their admiration, but his guests are hardly allowed time to furnish the plaudits demanded of them 'as every view was pointed out with a minuteness which left beauty entirely behind'. He can number the fields all around, and tell how many trees there are in the most distant clump. The prospect, however, which surpasses all others conceivable is that of Rosings glimpsed through an opening in the trees of its park.

Poor taste inheres perhaps less in weakness of judgment itself than in the distortion of judgment which considerations of wealth and gain bring about. And it takes on an infamous aspect when it applies itself to assessing motives and persons – as it does for Mr Collins in the charm and complaisance he finds in Lady Catherine. The same process is seen to affect the Miss Steeles in their estimation of those from whom they are likely to profit – where thrift, in other words, might follow fawning – or, for that matter, the whole population of Longbourn and Meryton at the appearance among them of a young man of great fortune. It operates within Charlotte Lucas, in her certainty that Elizabeth Bennet's dislike of the rich Mr Darcy will vanish if she once believes herself able to attract him. Most of all, it is in evidence in the avaricious John Dashwood. He eyes Colonel Brandon, on their first coming together at Mrs Jennings's, with a curiosity which seems to say that he only wants to know him rich, to be as civil to him as to the ladies. As he and Elinor set out for Conduit-street, where he has asked to be introduced, his first words as they leave the house are, 'Who is Colonel Brandon? Is he a man of fortune?' He confides to his sister that Mrs Jennings 'seems a most valuable woman indeed': her house and style of living 'all bespeak an exceeding good income', and the acquaintance may prove materially advantageous, as 'She must have a great deal to leave'. As they walk back, Elinor is assured he will have a charming account to carry to his wife: Lady Middleton is most elegant, and her mother 'an exceeding well-behaved woman, though not so elegant as her daughter'.

Fanny Dashwood will accept his appraisements without question: she has already shown her colours over the matter of her brother Edward's choice of a wife. And her mother is soon in like manner to establish the relative merits of Marianne's screen and Miss Morton's landscape by enunciating the principle, 'Miss Morton is Lord Morton's daughter.' But it is in John Dashwood that the ultimate declension is to be revealed. Colonel Brandon's gift of the living of Delaford to Edward Ferrars out of friendship and a desire to help evinces, in him, the shock of disbelief. The sale of the presentation might have brought fourteen hundred pounds if effected during the last incumbent's lifetime. '*Now* indeed it would be too late to sell it, but a man of Colonel Brandon's sense!' he exclaims. – 'I wonder he should be so improvident in a point of such common, such natural, concern! – Well, I am convinced there is a vast deal of inconsistency in almost every human character.' Motives of goodwill and generosity are beyond his awareness. The fact is a judgment: by it he is distanced from humanity just as surely as is an Iago.

It is no small tribute to Elizabeth Bennet, in an age so responsive to the vaunt of possession, that her calmness and independence of mind is unimpaired as she enters Rosings for the first time. Unlike her companions, she has the good taste that can contemplate the airs and appurtenances of privilege unmoved.

The persons of Jane Austen's novels are frequently observed to fail in one or other of the triplicity of needful qualities. It is their virtually complete absence in Mr Collins which makes him absurd; for in his mishaps in general he has much in common with his superiors. Yet he is not without a compensating excellence that deserves honourable mention, even if we do not find ourselves able to accord respect to its possessor. It has to do with his manner. The mistaken accusations Elizabeth directs at Darcy when he makes his proposal to her provoke in him resentment and recrimination in which the pretence of courtesy is dropped; at her statement of dislike he starts and is silent, looking at her with 'an expression of mingled incredulity and mortification'. But Mr Collins we never see taken aback: in time of crisis, urbanity does not desert him. The incivility to which Elizabeth is driven in rejecting his proposal moves him to compliment; the bitterness of failure reveals itself only in the increased fluency and heightened ceremoniousness of his address to Mrs Bennet.

This felicitous characteristic is shown more than once. It is present at the time of the *faux pas* at Netherfield, where Darcy greets his self-introduction with an unrestrained wonder that gives place successively to distant civility and unmasked contempt. That the affront has been sensed is evident from the nature of Mr Collins's ensuing speech to all and sundry. But on returning to Elizabeth he appears quite unruffled. He assures her he has no reason to be dissatisfied with the reception he has met: Darcy has been civil and even complimentary. 'Upon the whole,' he declares, 'I am much pleased with him.' The intimation is perhaps more than Elizabeth deserves, after having tried so strenuously to halt him in his intent. What she then has to say to him cannot be other than the reflection it is, but she is rebuffed in the kindest way imaginable: Mr Collins entertains the highest opinion in the world of her excellent judgment 'in all matters within the scope of your understanding', and seeks pardon for a neglect in this instance to profit by the advice which on every other subject will be his constant guide. The same beguiling complaisance is turned upon Elizabeth's father when, alarmed at the prospect of another visit, he attempts to dissuade his cousin by warning him, with unmistakable emphasis and iteration, not to risk the displeasure of his patroness by further absence. Having first thanked his host for the friendly caution and reassured him on this point, Mr Collins, no less determined to make use of Longbourn House for the continuance of his amours, is driven by the indignity to new altitudes of politeness. 'Believe me, my dear sir,' he cries, 'my gratitude is warmly excited by such affectionate attention; and depend upon it, you will speedily receive a letter of thanks for this, as well as for every other mark of your regard during my stay in Hertfordshire.'

Mr Collins is not too much of a fool to have feelings; and he is certainly no fool in the way in which he deals with insult by an enhancement of his customary courtesy. His manners may be too florid for elegance, too assiduous to be gentlemanly – but they are consistent. There is something here of a saving feature, especially for the era Mr Collins belongs to. The fellow has style.

9

Role

Is Jane Austen in any way a critic of the age she lived in? Like many others, David Cecil is convinced that she is not. Her standards, he writes in his admirable Life, were representative ones: she spoke for her times. Though she made no weak concession to convention, and always expressed her own thoughts, 'she happened to be born with a disposition naturally in sympathy with the point of view of the world in which she found herself.' Thus we do not encounter in her novels the aggressiveness of authors who feel themselves to be at odds with society: she writes with the wind behind her. Nor is there complaint or repining at the narrowness of the orthodox feminine world she knew as a woman and presents to us as a novelist.[1]

Certainly the stirring note of revolt is never sounded in her pages. But where else would one find so keen an eye for the tyrannies of wealth and rank, the injustices inherent in social position and the striving for it, the pitfalls of formal manners, or the plight of the necessitous man or dowerless woman, as these stories of attachment and marriage reveal? Is it possible that perspicacity of this order can stop short of the critical?

Lord David is guided by Jane Austen's own estimate of her vocation in affirming that she saw herself as an entertainer: that her primary motive in writing was not to edify, but to delight.[2] The same, though, might be said of Shakespeare, who worked under the far more urgent necessity of pleasing the many, but who brought to the task, as did she, a capacious intellect which must be always perceiving, beneath the 'plausive manners' of the life it experienced, the fabric and structure of the human condition itself. The conscious intention of such a writer need bear no relation to his achievement – for the further reason, no less operative in a product of the imagination, that, by the very nature of things, that can only entertain which bears affinity to truth. It was with this conviction that Sir Philip Sidney claimed as the function and end of his art 'that delightful teaching, which must be the right describing note to know a poet by'.[3] But all forms of literature instruct, and comedy not least.

It is certain, however, that Jane Austen, unlike the majority of authors, does not feel any need to insist, being confident always through a uniformity of culture of the sympathy of the minds for which she wrote. Thus she was against the avowedly instructive in a work of fiction, holding that example rather than direct approach is the true way for a novelist; and her stories, while naturally exemplifying her moral outlook, rarely moralise openly.[4] But this is not to gainsay the fact that the highest order of satirical writing seeks verisimilitude rather than exaggeration, chooses the reticent in preference to the declamatory. It allows motives and attributes to speak for themselves—for great artists have the means of presenting them in their immediacy and essence to the reader's apprehension. It is in Jane Austen's restraint, and her faithful depiction of manners, that her criticism of her age will be discerned, if it does indeed exist. She seems to accept the world as she finds it, and delineate it with vivid objectivity; yet her novels can be understood as a cry from the heart for sincerity, truth and fair dealing, and as a mute protest against the pretences and crudities, the injustices and slanders of the assured social order she knew.

In one respect, she could not take a critical attitude to personality without commenting on the world which produced it: for the social was to one of her upbringing and outlook inseparably part of human character. In his memorable nineteenth century analysis, Richard Simpson writes that man is known to her neither as possessor of a mystic individuality, nor as a composite of static qualities, but only in the process of his formation by social influences.

> She sees him, not as a solitary being completed in himself, but only as completed in society. Again, she contemplates virtues, not as fixed quantities, or as definable qualities, but as continual struggles and conquests, as progressive states of mind, advancing

by repulsing their contraries, or losing ground by being overcome. Hence again the individual mind can only be represented
by her as a battle-field where contending hosts are marshalled,
and where victory inclines now to one side and now to another.[5]

Personality in the novels arises out of the inward conflict of
pressures and principles, a strife in which all aspects of experience are necessarily comprised. The author thus can scarcely
lead us into finding fault with a character without social
reference or criticism being in some measure implied.

Society is in truth as much a protagonist, and as much under
surveillance, in Jane Austen's writing as the people of her
stories. But in this connection she has, according to D. W.
Harding, an interest more far-reaching and deeply subjective.
She is no reformer of society, and her object is not missionary; it
is 'the more desperate one of finding some mode of existence for
her critical attitudes'. It was essential for her to keep the
goodwill of those she associated with in everyday life; their
affection was important for her, and she had a profound respect
for the ordered society they upheld. Yet she was at the same time
so acutely sensitive to the harshnesses and complacencies of
which they were unaware as to know that she could only be
herself by resisting their values: and her novels are a way out of
the dilemma.[6] Her situation is one, as Mark Schorer explains,
'in which she was committed simultaneously to cherish and
abominate her world'; and she required as a novelist a technique which could both reveal and conceal: which could permit
her work to be enjoyed both in a trivial and a serious spirit,
according to the mind the reader brought to bear.[7] She is
prepared, therefore, to create characters, and even heroines,
who will have absorbed some of society's less edifying
possibilities.[8] This is the kind of undertaking she has in prospect
when announcing, 'I am going to take a heroine whom no one
but myself will much like.'[9]

That Emma's personality displays tendencies which the
author herself most disliked is beyond dispute: D.W. Harding
instances the self-conceit, the patronising pleasure in meddling
in the lives of others, and the inveterate snobbery. These things
are indefensible; but in them, and the prejudices and cruelties

inherent in them, the heroine is a representative young gentle-woman of her age: her superiority, real or assumed, is based upon the values of the society she patronises.[10] The failings are however not immediately apparent, but are overlaid by what is substantial and endearing in Emma's nature. As Harding puts it, 'instead of being attributed in exaggerated form to a character distanced in caricature, they occur in the subtle forms given them by someone who in many ways has admittedly fine standards.'[11] The novel is thus a progress towards what he calls the 'humbling self-effacement' of its heroine. Its structure accommodates what is elsewhere seen as a necessary loss and gain: there is a twofold movement in which Emma suffers reduction in the social scale by her failures amongst others and her humiliating discoveries about herself, while at the same time growing to true stature from the moral viewpoint. She has acquired through her nurturing the self-importance, egotism, and even malice which are a reflection of the social order; the story shows her moving towards recognition, liberation and full selfhood in the course of settling more completely into her society.[12]

Emma's achievement, though, does not concern herself alone. Her disengagement from its dis-naturing pressures implies a criticism of the order she lives under; but her conduct with regard to Harriet Smith is little short of being an outright denunciation. It contradicts both her customary attitude and judgments and those of society. For Harriet is a nobody whom Emma persists in thinking capable of advancement, and of marriage to a man of respectability, if not of distinction. Is she a romantic or a realist? And, in the situation which the author has created, is the point of view being expressed Jane Austen's or Emma's? Harriet is debarred from marrying Mr Elton, and Jane Fairfax forbidden to Frank Churchill, upon considerations in differing proportion of status and finance; but in other respects the unions are manifestly desirable. Harriet, as Emma recog-nises, would have been a better match for Mr Elton than Augusta Hawkins. These anomalies are puzzling, and have led one critic to declare that 'Jane Austen seems not quite sure what we should think on such matters'. Though the marriages that do take place are suitable, he writes, there is several times to be found, particularly in Emma's conversation with the low-born and illegitimate Harriet, 'a certain freedom of opinion which is surprising'; and he finds it impossible 'to conclude precisely what were Jane Austen's opinions on these matters'.[13] His failure is due to the good reason that she is exercising the restraint and displaying the empathy of the true artist; but he has been disturbed, as it was doubtless intended he should be, by a criticism of the conventions as powerful as it is implicit.

The hollowness of the claims of class and wealth and the arbitrariness of traditional values are frequently exposed in the novels – whether in Sir Walter Elliot's disparagement of the Navy 'as being the means of bringing persons of obscure birth into undue distinction', or in Elizabeth Bennet's denouncing coming out as an abuse, her indignation against the moneyed yet ill-bred Bingley sisters, and her sardonic question to Colonel Fitzwilliam. Elizabeth's contempt for the claims of birth and riches which form impediments to the marriage of true minds, to sincerity of dealing and to the just estimation of worth, is Jane Austen's own. And through purposeful use of the character of Emma, she makes the point with even greater emphasis.

The novel proves Harriet's native reputableness and merit. She may be a numbskull – but she is a person: a creature of instinctive kindness, decent feelings and warmth of heart. At the beginning, Emma asserts playfully to Mr Knightley that, if he were ever to marry, Harriet would be the right woman for him; as the tale nears its end, she and the reader are aware of the plausibility and proprieties of so unusual a match. Jane Austen may be said to have written *Pygmalion* a century before Bernard Shaw did – with the same effect of bringing to light the abuses and detractions rife within the social order, though not with a reformer's purpose. She is in a way more practical than he: more conscious of her character's human limitations, and of the reality of the strengths, and the merits, of her society. But in the involvements of Harriet Smith a radical criticism of the established order is conveyed; and in Emma herself, through the deliberate uniting of opposed principles – a thoroughgoing snobbery and an impossible romanticism – the criticism is embodied. Margaret Kennedy tells us that 'Warm feeling is ever the good angel in Miss Austen's stories. Her characters are at their best when advised by their hearts, and most of their errors come from their heads.'[14] When Emma puts her preconceptions aside and is advised by her heart, the disabling assumptions, the snobberies and the inhumanities which have been engrafted upon her own personality – and for which society rather than the heroine is to be blamed – disappear.

This intensification of a character's social conditioning for the purposes of a critical, and indeed a satirical, art is of course found in Lady Catherine de Bourgh, who is the arrogance of rank personified. But it is also found in her nephew. The intriguing parallel existing between Mr Darcy and Mr Collins, evident in their ways of courtship – and perhaps most clearly so in the pronouncements upon its object's inferiority of connection by the one, and of wealth by the other – extends to their characters. Each expresses his inmost sentiments with vigour and abandon. In Darcy we are given a man to whom disguise of any sort is abhorrent: in Mr Collins, a man who is almost incapable of any sort of disguise. Both contrive to exasperate Elizabeth Bennet; but that someone of Darcy's pretension should do so by his mode of address, in the very process of asking for his lady's hand, is a circumstance truly remarkable. Its strangeness does not escape Elizabeth. When Darcy complains at the uncompromisingness of the negative which has greeted his speech, she is driven to inquire 'why with so evident a design of offending and insulting me, you chose to tell me that you liked me against your will, against your reason, and even against your character? Was not this some excuse for incivility, if I *was* uncivil?'

It was more than excuse: it was invitation. And its oddity suggests to Richard Simpson that the author, in constructing her chief characters, 'sometimes lets her theory run away with her'. His argument is very much to the point.

> Darcy, in *Pride and Prejudice*, is the proud man; but he is a gentleman by birth and education, and a gentleman in feeling. Would it be possible for such a man, in making a proposal of marriage to a lady whose only fault in his eyes is that some of her connections are vulgar, to do so in the way in which Darcy makes

his overtures to Elizabeth? It is true that great pains are taken to explain this wonderful lapse of propriety. But, all the explanations notwithstanding, an impression is left on the reader that either Darcy is not so much of a gentleman as he is represented, or that his conduct is forced a little beyond the line of nature in order the better to illustrate the theory of his biographer.[15]

Margaret Kennedy is also disturbed at Darcy's uncouthness – so much so, that she is tempted into overstatement, and is ready to think that he 'only exists to play scenes with Elizabeth', despite elsewhere finding him real and convincing. And she notes that the inadmissible conduct is not confined to this scene, but that 'his extreme insolence, at the first Meryton ball, does not match his later behaviour'.[16]

It is indeed the 'theory of his biographer' which produces this swerving from the natural line into inconsistency – for Darcy is at these moments the embodiment of the social vices she deplores. With literary skill, and depth of human understanding, she makes him conscious of his inadequacy, and its cause. As an only son, he confides to Elizabeth at the end, he was spoilt by a father and mother who, though good themselves, 'allowed, encouraged, almost taught me to be selfish and overbearing, to care for none beyond my own family circle, to think meanly of the rest of the world, to *wish* at least to think meanly of their sense and worth compared with my own.' His parents, in fact, combined the stature of Sir Thomas Bertram with the illiberality of Mrs Norris. This might explain his rudeness to Elizabeth at the ball – but it can never excuse the manner of his wooing. For to a degree Darcy is there the expression of social trends and forces which Jane Austen deprecates. At that point, as well as being himself, he is a device of the satirist.

As he is during that visit to Hunsford Parsonage, so is the incumbent of the parish all the time. Aspects of ills social and human are of course to be found distributed in greater or lesser measure in the make-up of the persons of the novels. But it is possible for a writer to make a more thorough representation, and place much or all in a single character.

A happening of this kind occurs, with pathetic and terrible import, amidst the surges of tragic disillusionment in *King Lear*.

Bereft now of kingdom and kindred, and defenceless against the storm on the heath, Lear has turned a revivified intellect upon himself and the world. The fugitive Edgar, in his disguise as the beggar Poor Tom, suddenly appears before him out of the roaring darkness. Fear of his pursuers obliges him to persist in his role, and in demented chattering declare himself a former serving-man, 'proud in heart and mind; that curl'd my hair; wore gloves in my cap; serv'd the lust of my mistress' heart, and did the act of darkness with her; swore as many oaths as I spake words, and broke them in the sweet face of Heaven'. But under the inexorable demands of drama and of truth, he is soon blazoning forth the fact of man's depraved condition, as one who by ingenerate instinct is 'false of heart, light of ear, bloody of hand; hog in sloth, fox in stealth, wolf in greediness, dog in madness, lion in prey'. The old King, with inspired imagination bordering upon insanity, sees in the trembling wretch who confronts him the key to the mystery, both of his present plight and his former self-deception. Triumphantly, he greets him with the cry, 'thou art the thing itself; unaccommodated man is no more but such a poor, bare, forked animal as thou art.'

Thus it is – in similar fashion, but markedly unlike effect – with Lady Catherine's protégé. The failings, not of mankind, but of the society Jane Austen understood so well, are here 'attributed in exaggerated form to a character distanced in caricature'. Mr Collins is the living expression and microcosm of all those things against which her soul is in revolt, but with which she must in her personal life come to terms: her world's brittle elegance and dominating materialism, its pomposities and pretensions, its unfeelingness and inhumanities, its stupidities and its mindlessness. Throughout the novel she points an accusatory finger at their besotted embodiment, and declaims, 'Thou art the thing itself!'

This representative role means that despite his position in *Pride and Prejudice*, Mr Collins remains a flat character. He does not develop, because he may not. Elizabeth, on arriving at Hunsford, predictably finds him unaltered; and one must be glad that, in this instance, time and circumstance will never take their usual toll.

Mr Collins is an expedient to which his creator did not afterwards have recourse. But her own attitude, and the art which was born of it, is constant. It is Jane Austen's critical gaze which gives potency and actuality to her characterisation. For the more one knows human nature, the more one realises how grievously it is flawed; and to write with understanding and kindness does not preclude a sensitivity to shortcoming, but requires it. Can the lively similitude of persons ever be fully attained where the writer's outlook is limited to the mortal scene? One suspects not. In the last resort, only a universality of awareness can set humanity in perspective. What is true of normal living applies with peculiar force to the creation of life-like characters. The proper study of mankind is man: but the task will never near completion until vision extends beyond him and gains some ultimate point of reference. Jane Austen's distinction in character-creation implies this further accomplishment; nor is it here without significance that her criticism is of a quality at once more incisive and more gentle than that of the ordinary satirist of mankind.

In being the target for her ironic humour, Mr Collins is unremarkable, for she aims at all her characters. She consciously seeks in the novels to clarify the means of happiness in the social context; but the source of her criticism is far removed from a human society of whose follies and inadequacies she is painfully but resignedly aware. We surely hear the author's own voice – that of a mature perception – in Elizabeth's reaction to Jane's trying to praise her.

> 'Do not be afraid of my running into any excess, of my encroaching on your privilege of universal good will. You need not. There are few people whom I really love, and still fewer of whom I think well. The more I see of the world, the more I am dissatisfied with it; and every day confirms my belief of the inconsistency of all human characters, and of the little dependence that can be placed on the appearance of either merit or sense.'

This is dissatisfaction severe enough to incur the title of

disillusionment. And it may be judged to stem, as is properly the case, from an elevated sense both of rightness itself and of human potentiality. David Cecil tells how he became convinced, in preparing Jane Austen's biography, that faith was an element in her life of the greatest significance, and that her moral views corresponded entirely, if unobtrusively, with her personal practice of religion and the interpretations of the Anglican Church.[17] Glimpses – but no more – reach us from the Letters: in the advice to Fanny Knight not to be frightened by the idea of her suitor John Plumtre acting 'more strictly up to the precepts of the New Testament than others', since 'Wisdom is better than Wit, & in the long run will certainly have the laugh on her side';[18] or her wish that Sir John Moore, in his last words at Corunna, had united 'something of the Christian with the Hero in his death';[19] or the tailpiece of a letter to her niece Anna Austen: 'I am very fond of Sherlock's Sermons, prefer them to almost any.'[20] But more illuminating still is her reference to the 'sad story about Mrs Powlett', a former neighbour at Steventon, in whose elopement from her husband a certain Lord S. had been implicated. Her words are startling in the meaning they carry. 'I should not have suspected her of such a thing. – She staid the Sacrament I remember, the last time that you & I did.'[21] The comment, in its ingenuousness and absoluteness, brings into view the very nerve and fibre of devotion – and indicates the origin of that heightened moral sensitivity which can view the worldly scene with such disenchantment, such tolerance, such humour, and such stark clarity. For her notions of human potential derived from the New Testament's hero, and her principles from what was revealed in its story.

Her attitude to her fellow men and women was that of Isabella in *Measure for Measure* – and thus, who knows? possibly Shakespeare's own. She saw that the creature man, inflexible in proud aversion from his being's source and end,

> Dress'd in a little brief authority,
> Most ignorant of what he's most assur'd –
> His glassy essence – like an angry ape
> Plays such fantastic tricks before high heaven
> As makes the angels weep; who, with our spleens,
> Would all themselves laugh mortal.

Some such high-wrought apprehension, such transfiguring vision of human existence *sub specie aeternitatis*, one can be sure lies behind Shakespeare's achievement in comedy and tragedy alike. Jane Austen is purely the comedian. Possessing our own spleen, she received with delight the absurdity and inconsistency of her fellows, and proceeded to immortalise it with genius unrivalled in her craft. Yet her soul, though not his equal in creativity, was in scope no less comprehensive than her master's. What gives acuteness and authority to her observation of persons is acquaintance with the tragic aspect of life. And in the poignancy of the secular situations she sets before us, and of the human inadequacies they reveal, we may find the angelic dismay, sorrow and compassion.

Notes

Chapter 1   Query

1 Margaret Kennedy, *Jane Austen*, The Novelists Series, Arthur Barker, 2nd edn, 1957, p. 61.
2 'Trollope on *Emma*: an unpublished note', *Nineteenth Century Fiction*, IV, Berkeley and Los Angeles, University of California Press, 1949, pp. 246–7.
3 Sir W. Scott, review of *Emma*, *Quarterly Review*, XIV, 1815, p. 200.
4 Lionel Trilling, '*Emma* and the legend of Jane Austen', *Beyond Culture*, London, Secker & Warburg, 1966, p. 47.
5 Kennedy, op. cit., pp. 64–5.
6 David Cecil, *A Portrait of Jane Austen*, London, Constable, 1978, pp. 156–7.
7 Kennedy, op. cit., p. 84.
8 Ibid., p. 92.
9 Trilling, op. cit., p. 48.

Chapter 2   Compliment

1 R. W. Chapman (ed.), *Jane Austen's Letters to her Sister Cassandra and Others*, London, Oxford University Press, 1932, p. 93: Thursday 20 November 1800.

Chapter 4   Wealth

1 David Cecil, *A Portrait of Jane Austen,* London, Constable, 1978, p. 76.
2 Arnold Kettle, *An Introduction to the English Novel,* I, London, Hutchinson, 1967, p. 92.
3 Mark Schorer, 'The humiliation of Emma Woodhouse', *The Literary Review*, Teaneck, New Jersey, Fairleigh Dickinson University, II, no. 4,

1959, pp. 548–50; reprinted in David Lodge (ed.), *Jane Austen: 'Emma'*, Casebook Series, London, Macmillan, 1968, pp. 171–3.
4 W. H. Auden, 'Letter to Lord Byron', I, *Collected Longer Poems*, London, Faber & Faber, 1968, p. 41.

Chapter 5   Station

1 Jerome K. Jerome, *The Idle Thoughts of an Idle Fellow*, London, Field & Tuer, 1886, pp. 25–6.

Chapter 6   Colloquy

1 J. Boswell, *Life of Johnson*, 3rd edn (ed. J.D. Fleeman), London, Oxford University Press, 1970, p. 623: Friday 14 April 1775.

Chapter 7   Romance

1 David Cecil, *A Portrait of Jane Austen*, London, Constable, 1978, p. 161.
2 See R.W. Chapman's note: *The Novels of Jane Austen*, 3rd edn, V, London, Oxford University Press, 1933, p. 269. The 1818 text, in which these two sentences constitute one speech, clearly errs in giving Thorpe as the speaker. Chapman's expedient of making each sentence a separate speech, with Thorpe uttering the reflection on Catherine in the second, seems questionable in terms of that gentleman's relationship to the Morlands, and his subsequently becoming the lady's suitor. The speech is here taken to be an outburst of the kind not unknown within families, similar to that of Mrs Bennet with regard to her 'headstrong foolish' second daughter.
3 Cecil, op. cit., p. 16.

Chapter 8   Dearth

1 David Cecil, *A Portrait of Jane Austen*, London, Constable, 1978, p. 149.
2 Ibid.

Chapter 9   Role

1 David Cecil, *A Portrait of Jane Austen*, London, Constable, 1978, pp. 68, 150.
2 Ibid., p. 151.
3 Sir P. Sidney, *Defence of Poesy*, iv.
4 Cecil, op. cit., p. 151.
5 Richard Simpson, 'Jane Austen', *North British Review*, XXCII, 1870, p. 137.
6 D.W. Harding, 'Regulated hatred: an aspect of the work of Jane Austen', *Scrutiny*, VIII, 1940, p. 351.
7 Mark Schorer, 'The humiliation of Emma Woodhouse', *The Literary Review*, Teaneck, New Jersey, Fairleigh Dickinson University, II, no. 4, 1959, p. 554; reprinted in David Lodge (ed.), *Jane Austen: 'Emma'*, Casebook Series, London, Macmillan, 1968, pp. 177–8.
8 Harding, op. cit., p. 359.
9 J.E. Austen Leigh, *A Memoir of Jane Austen*, 3rd edn, London, Richard Bentley & Son, 1872, p. 148; ed. R.W. Chapman, Oxford, Clarendon Press, 1926, p. 157.
10 Marvin Mudrick, *Jane Austen: Irony as Defense and Discovery*, Princeton, New Jersey, Princeton University Press, 1952, p. 184.
11 Harding, op. cit., p. 360.
12 Schorer, op. cit., pp. 551–2; Lodge (ed.), op. cit., p. 175.
13 E.N. Hayes, '*Emma*: a dissenting opinion', *Nineteenth Century Fiction*, IV, Berkeley and Los Angeles, University of California Press, 1949, p. 7.
14 M. Kennedy, *Jane Austen*, The Novelists Series, London, Arthur Barker, 2nd edn, 1957, p. 59.
15 R. Simpson, op. cit., pp. 149–50.
16 Kennedy, op. cit., p. 60.
17 Cecil, op. cit., p. 50. See the testimony of Henry Austen in his Biographical Note of the Author prefaced to the 1818 edition of *Northanger Abbey* and *Persuasion*.
18 R.W. Chapman (ed.), *Jane Austen's Letters to her Sister Cassandra and Others*, London, Oxford University Press, 1932, p. 410: Friday 18 November 1814.
19 Ibid., p. 261: Monday 30 January 1809.
20 Ibid., p. 406: Wednesday 28 September 1814.
21 Ibid., p. 197: Monday 20 June 1808.

Index

Allen, Mr, 13, 25–6, 42, 126
Allen, Mrs, 13, 25–6, 43, 126
Andrews, Miss, 70
attachment and courtship: deceptive medium, 89–91, 96–9, 120–31; encouragement and 'particularity', 91–110, 120, 122–3; guardedness and reserve, 91–6, 110–13; inadvertence and unguardedness, 96, 99–110, 120–3; marriage, 115–19, 126–30, 131–40; romance, 17–21, 75–81, 91–6, 106–7, 115–16, 130–7; *see also* Austen, Jane; Bennet, Elizabeth; Collins, Mr; proposals and declarations; 'prudence'; wealth and marriage; women in society
Auden, W.H., 52
Austen, Anna, 162
Austen, Jane: author's comment, 9–10, 28, 94, 126, 136, 160–1; characterisation, 2–5, 160–2; faith, 161–3; heart, qualities of, 145, 147, 158; *Letters*, 12, 162; rank and wealth, 33, 49, 56–7, 160; romance, 78, 92, 106–7, 132–3, 136–7; satire, 7, 12, 154–63; social forms, 12, 20, 32–3, 38–9, 51–2, 106–7, 126–30, 153–61; women, 49, 94, 106–7, 115–16, 134–5

Bates, Miss Hetty, 3, 71, 72, 81, 145
Bennet, Elizabeth: criticism and contention, 7–9, 19–20, 23, 41, 49, 87, 103–8, 113, 151; discernment and intelligence, 3, 5–9, 10, 22–3, 29, 44–5, 49, 50, 52, 60–1, 72, 82, 83–4, 87, 92, 94, 100, 106–7, 123, 127, 135, 138, 140, 144, 161; error, 6–8, 61, 94, 107, 124, 125, 134–5; humour, 20, 23, 49, 60, 82, 88, 100, 103, 104–5; rank and wealth, attitude to, 36–7, 47–50, 60–2, 134–5, 149, 150, 157; relation to Mr Collins, 5–9, 23, 34, 52, 53, 54, 55, 63–5, 82–5, 88–90, 95–6, 98, 100–1, 112–13, 119, 122, 131, 144, 151, 160; relation to Mr Darcy, 1, 18–20, 43–4, 47–8, 49–50, 54, 59–62, 68, 89, 90, 97, 101–8, 111–12, 124, 136–7, 151, 158–9; unguardedness, 101–8, 110, 122; *other*, 3, 11, 15, 31, 41, 45, 62, 70, 82, 83, 130, 141, 149
Bennet, Jane, 5–8, 15, 22–3, 36, 48, 52, 59, 60, 74, 93, 94, 123–4, 131, 135, 140, 144, 161
Bennet, Lydia, 37, 41, 82, 84–5, 136, 137–8, 139–41
Bennet, Mary, 85
Bennet, Mr William, 1, 5, 9, 11–12, 41, 49, 50, 51, 52, 65, 66, 82, 83, 84–5, 113, 124, 127, 128, 137, 138, 140–1, 142, 144, 148, 151–2
Bennet, Mrs, 50, 65, 82, 84, 86, 93, 105–6, 113, 124, 127, 131, 138, 140, 151

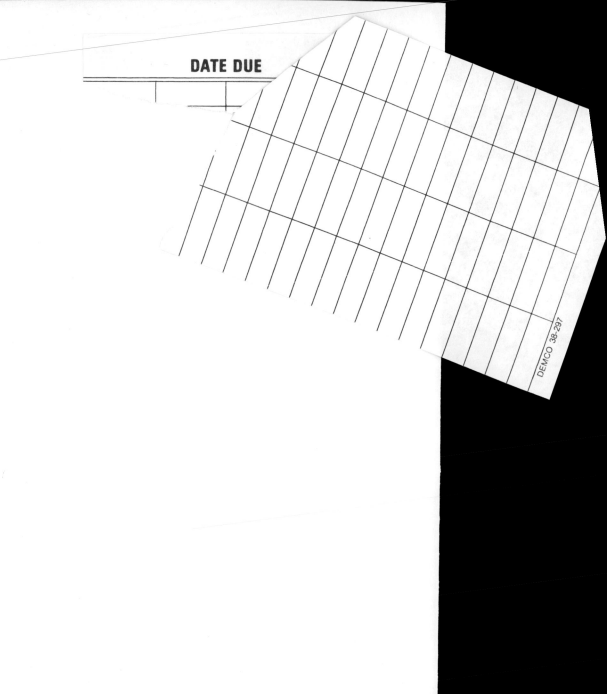

DATE DUE

DEMCO 38-297